CW00540802

THE GREATEST POLICEMAN?

A BIOGRAPHY OF
CAPT. ATHELSTAN POPKESS CBE, OStJ

Chief Constable of
Nottingham City Police 1930-1959

TOM ANDREWS

BLUE LAMP
BOOKS

ISBN: 978-1-911273-89-9 (hardcover)
ISBN: 978-1-911273-90-5 (ebook)

Published by Blue Lamp Books

An imprint of
Mango Books

18 Soho Square
London W1D 3QL

www.MangoBooks.co.uk

THE GREATEST POLICEMAN?

This book is dedicated to my wife Katie
and children Danny and Josie,
who have allowed me the time
to indulge my hobby.

Contents

In Memoriam of

The Police Historian Richard Cowley, who sadly passed away in 2016. It was his suggestion that I write an article about Captain Popkess for the *Journal of the Police History Society* set me down this path.

Retired Chief Superintendent Dennis Silverwood QPM who sadly passed away in January 2018 after having given me a fascinating and unique insight into The Captain but before I had finished this book.

*

I would also like to take this opportunity to thank John Andrews, who took a lot of time to proof-read and offer feedback on my initial drafts, and Sue Andrews for all her support and encouragement. Thank you to Bob Rosamund, retired City Police officer and source of many anecdotes, for giving up his time, and providing follow-up support to me throughout the lengthy writing of this book.

I would also like to thank my colleague and fellow police history fanatic Rob Phillips, who joined me interviewing Dennis Silverwood and several former female police officers for a separate project.

Thanks must also go to Clive Emsley and Chris Williams of the Open University who assisted me via email.

Finally a huge thank you to the committee of the Police History Society who have supported the progress of this book, as well as Adam Wood at Blue Lamp Books who agreed to take on this novice's first work and all the work he has done to get it into print.

FOREWORD

Clive Emsley

Boys (and tomboys) growing up in the inter-war years and the years shortly after the Second World War were urged to read what were known as 'Ripping Yarns.' These told the stories of imperial heroes; the men who kept order to distant parts of the Empire. These places were not yet the Commonwealth, they were simply the rugged, dangerous jungles of Africa and India, with rugged and dangerous populations.

No-one would write such stories today; at least not with the same backdrops of dangers both human and animal. Such 'heroes' would appear make-believe not to mention embarrassing, and perhaps racist too. Yet Athelstan Popkess, with his mixture of an Anglo-Saxon and Victorian name remains the apogee of such a 'hero'.

Tom Andrews has done a valuable job in this book, bringing Popkess to life. Moreover, however the modern reader views the man, there can be no doubting his courage as a soldier and the ability and intelligence that he brought to the development of policing during his life.

Popkess was a child of empire, so it is hardly surprising that he should have acted as he did in his youth. What is, perhaps, more surprising is that after a serious wound he should have been so keen to get back to the battlefield. After service in the First World War he opted to join the auxiliary Black and Tans during the war in Ireland, and then he served in Palestine. The 'Tans' have a grim reputation and so too does the Palestine Gendarmerie, two reasons, in addition to his lack of police service, why there was reluctance to see him promoted to Chief Constable of Nottingham in 1930. Yet as Andrews shows, over the next twenty-nine years Popkess proved himself to be a significant reformer of police and policing.

Popkess was keen to promote big men for his force. He was particularly keen to have the centre of Nottingham patrolled by former guardsmen often well-over six-feet who, he believed, could keep order and warn off any likely offenders. His most significant achievements as Chief Constable, however, were various improvements on the roads, on drivers' behaviour and awareness, the deployment of traffic wardens, and burglar alarms linked to the police. Equally significant was some of the first use of forensic science when the topic remained in its infancy and most forces largely ignored it.

While he may have had military roots, Popkess showed himself to be an able police chief; one that thought carefully and significantly about the job. Andrews is good on this, and he is also good on showing how Popkess could easily rub people up the wrong way. His fascination with sport, particularly boxing, led to him to taking a team to Nazi Germany and infuriating liberal Englishmen with a Nazi salute before a match involving the men from his force. While some protested Popkess was not a Nazi, he was blunt and at times difficult. He organised air-raid precautions efficiently and effectively. But in the aftermath of the war Popkess again infuriated the dominant Labour group in Nottingham when he sought to prosecute some dubious behaviour on their part. Popkess was in the right and was noted as such by the powers that be, but he was a crotched and difficult individual who was always determined to press his case. Eventually the Association of Chief Police Officers stepped in with moderating words and the financial wherewithal to pay off his solicitor's bill, which ended concerns of dirty linen being washed in public and also, perhaps, any public blemish on Popkess's reputation. Andrews does not mention it, but it also seems likely that the death of Popkess's wife shortly before the clash with local government, together with his hard, if colourful life, may have led him with some form of breakdown.

Some might query the idea of Popkess as 'the Greatest Policeman', if only because of his difficult and fearsome behaviour towards the Nottingham Council. Yet his role in scientific policing and in the development of roads and motor traffic was significant. In this day and age there will be some who, foolishly, insist on ignoring a man because he seems to have been tainted with racism. But it is impossible to remove a man from his time, and difficult to cut him away from the thinking of his day. Unquestionably, few before or since have had such an influence on policing in such a formative time as Athelstan Popkess.

INTRODUCTION

Captain Athelstan Horn Popkess may sound like a character from an 18th century melodrama, but in this case the truth is even better than fiction. This man, with such an unusual name, in fact deserves to be recognised as one of the most influential figures in the history of British policing.

Where Sir Robert Peel gets the credit for founding the police service, the man at the helm of Nottingham City Police for nearly three decades from 1930 to 1959 single-handedly pioneered many of the techniques that transformed the service into what we recognise today. For this, until now, he has received little to no credit. This book seeks to undo this injustice, and highlight the staggering influence cast by Popkess that continues to this day, more than half a century after his retirement. In fact, some of the innovations pioneered by Popkess are so ingrained in modern policing methods that it is almost impossible to think that they had been 'invented' at all.

Popkess was not Britain's youngest-ever British Chief Constable when commencing his post with Nottingham City Police at aged 37; far from it, in fact. In 1842 the Nottinghamshire Constabulary appointed the 22-year-old Peter Hatton as Chief Constable,[1] and

Captain Athelstan Popkess

one (disputed) claimant from Rochdale Borough Police reckons to have been only 20 on his appointment in 1863. Nor does Capt. Popkess' 29 years at the helm of Nottingham's city force make him anywhere near being Britain's longest serving Chief Constable. That accolade goes to a Chief with twice as much service at the reins of a force.[2] He certainly wasn't the only Chief to receive a King or Queen's Police Medal, which seems to be part of the trappings of office for the rank; and he also wasn't the only one to be inducted into various heraldic orders either. He wasn't Nottingham City Police's first or last Chief Constable, and he wasn't responsible for its amalgamation with Nottinghamshire (County) Constabulary, which occurred nine years after his retirement (and a year after his death).

It was his innovations in policing methodology and working practices that mark Popkess as such an influential figure in policing history. The Nottingham City Police force under his stewardship was the first to introduce, pioneer or help legislate for an incredible list of things such as:

- Mobile vehicle patrols
- Police radio communications
- Police driving standards
- Sirens on police vehicles
- Drink driving legislation
- Road safety and accident prevention

1   Clark, Peter B.H. "Who was the Youngest Chief Constable?" in *The Journal of the Police History Society* Number 30: 2016 p. 81

2   Cowley, Richard. *A History of the British Police: From its Earliest Beginnings to the Present Day*. Gloucestershire: The History Press (2011) pp. 154-159

- Traffic wardens
- Air-raid prevention and safety
- Forensic science
- The removal of politics from policing
- Driving theory and hazard perception tests
- Burglar alarms linked directly to the police
- Radar speed traps (speed cameras)

This list is far from exhaustive, and it was with these accomplishments that Popkess made the small provisional borough force Nottingham City Police the example to beat in the field of policing. As one retired officer who served under Popkess put it:

> "It was known that Nottingham City Police was the best in the country, and possibly the world. Anyone who wanted to be a policeman in a decent force wanted to come to Nottingham. People came from other forces to come to Nottingham."

In recognition of his innovating, his work with regards to road safety and his leading Nottingham City Police to being such an exemplar in the field of policing, Popkess was progressively made an Officer of the Most Excellent Order of the British Empire (OBE), and then a Commander of the same Order (CBE) in 1955. He was also inducted into the Knightly Order of Saint John in recognition for his work reducing road casualties and deaths and improving safety, earning him the post nominals CBE and OStJ.[3]

---

3   *The London Gazette* supplement 34469 31st December 1937 pp. 19; *The London Gazette* supplement 40669 30th December 1955 pp. 12; *The London Gazette* supplement 41764 14th July 1959 p. 4469

Perhaps his most important legacy is the one for which he is almost exclusively remembered. It was also probably the only one he didn't set out to achieve. This was to confirm the independence of the police from political interference.

The national unease following the Chief Constable's suspension by the Nottingham City Council towards the end of his tenure sparked a public outrage that culminated in parliamentary debates and a Royal Commission into Policing. This ultimately fixed the police as answerable to local and national government, but not directly controlled by them, supporting Popkess' contention.

The 'Popkess Affair', as it came to be known, was sparked by an allegation of corruption amongst local councillors, and brought about a notorious conclusion to an illustrious career. It was to set a precedent which has helped make policing in Britain the envy of many other countries in the world.

A politically-motivated complaint of corruption was made regarding a senior councillor, which Popkess was duty bound to investigate. The allegation was made by a prospective local MP in an effort to blacken the name of his rivals. The investigation caused much chagrin within the Nottingham City Council, who at that time were responsible for overseeing the local police force. Popkess was undone by the political powers of the very man he was requested to investigate, ultimately finding himself suspended from his role as Chief Constable by the Watch Committee, of which his suspect was a member. This was further compounded by a clash of personalities between Popkess and the Council's senior legal advisor.

Popkess, however, had a strong character with a powerful sense of right and wrong, forged during his youth on the wild plains of

South Africa and Rhodesia. His childhood, examined further in the chapter 'Making the Man', was one that not even Kipling could have dreamt up. His sense of morality was further honed during his time as an officer on the African front in the First World War, where he witnessed brutal close-quarters combat, and then time serving in Ireland as a military intelligence officer during the uprising in which atrocities were committed by both sides. A war of words and deeds against minor bureaucrats was not something from which Popkess would back down.

Popkess' position was that he would not hand over notes on his investigation to the very person he was investigating, even in the face of the threat of his career. This stance was ultimately ratified by no lesser a person than the Home Secretary. Popkess was vindicated, but at a significant personal cost to a man who on the outside was a South African lion, but inside may have already been hugely troubled by the black dog of depression, as shall be seen in the chapter 'Controversies'.

Ending in controversy and a run-in with the City Council, Popkess' career had started in the same vein. Popkess was an interloper to his position when he was appointed in 1930. Perhaps the most influential figure in policing should never have got the job in the first place. By this time in his life he had also narrowly cheated death more times that should be reasonable, and so was incredibly lucky to even be alive, let alone in a position to apply.

A short-list of three more qualified candidates had been drawn up for the vacant Nottingham City Police Chief Constable position in 1930, on which Popkess did not feature. A bizarre last-minute addition in still relatively unknown circumstances, Popkess had no policing background to speak of, in spite of that being a legal requirement for the role. Awarded the post by the

Watch Committee, the City Council objected and once again it took intervention by the Home Secretary, initiated through an unannounced visit by Popkess, to confirm his appointment.

This proactive visit by Popkess to the Home Secretary gives an insight into the drive and ambition of a man who was to transform policing through his desire to make it as efficient and organised as possible. He was able to do this in part from the strict discipline he imposed on the Nottingham City force, as well as his very militaristic outlook on recruitment. He was barely seen by his subordinates, instead letting his senior officers run the force, a former officer Bob Rosamund who served under Popkess recalls:

> "He was very careful about choosing his senior staff, but when they were in post, he let them get on with it. I never saw him outside of his office. I only ever met him that once [on my first day at work]. Discipline was strict, but it never [reached] him, it was dealt with by Superintendents."

The best people to help paint the most complete picture of Popkess were those who worked with him and for him, and the views of the rank and file officers of 'The Captain' (as they reverentially referred to him) are just as important as the strategic look at his influence and legacy. These officers' opinions are the ones which newspapers, newsreels and other accounts of the time do not capture, but demonstrate a key alternative view and insight into what made the man so important, and form an important part of social history.

Far and away the best source about Popkess, however, is the man himself. He wrote extensively both about his own life and on diverse policing topics, and this pantheon of work forms a large part of what makes him so influential. Not only did he pioneer new methods, but he shared these initiatives with his peers in trade journals to improve the police nationally. These writings allow us to far more comprehensively understand his thought processes and goals for the police. Equally as important in helping gain an understanding of what made him the man and leader he was is the autobiography of his early life *Sweat in my Eyes*, published in 1952 whilst still serving as Chief Constable, and its follow-up *Guns in the Sun*, published under his later pen name, Bardo Kidogo.

Sadly both these autobiographies only cover a period long before his policing career, in spite of having been written towards the end of his time as Chief. Perhaps a misguided sense of modesty around his role as Chief Constable, coupled with the controversies he experienced towards the end of his time, dissuaded him from writing about his period in Nottingham City Police. Certainly the way his career ended, coupled with the depression he was suffering from at this point in his life, would have seriously deterred him from dragging up perhaps painful memories.

The first chapter, 'Making the Man', provides a summary of this childhood and early pre-policing career, in order to set the scene for his tenure as Nottingham's 'top cop' and examine how and why he formed the character that drove him to this position.

The rest of this book will explore Capt. Popkess' time as Chief Constable thematically, looking at his achievements, initiatives and aims individually, rather than simply presenting a chronological narrative of his time of service.

Helping to complete this look into Popkess' service, three retired officers who served alongside and under him as Chief Constable have provided their memories of the force at the time, and specifically what life was like under his stewardship. Former PCs Bob Rosamund and Mary Needham both provided the author with various anecdotes and background information; and perhaps most crucially former Chief Superintendent Dennis Silverwood – who served as Popkess' staff officer for many years – provided in depth insight into some lesser known aspects of Popkess' tenure.

These contributions, especially those of Silverwood who worked so closely under Popkess and who went on to senior rank, in part he states due to the guidance and the lessons he learned around leadership that Popkess gave him, are crucial in showing the true nature of the man. Without the contribution of Dennis Silverwood, Popkess' depression would almost certainly have never been known about. A very private man, he managed to largely hide his condition from everyone, with the assistance of his senior officers. It was only Silverwood's position as his staff officer and perhaps almost friend and confidante, that meant he was able to see him during these dark periods when Popkess was largely absent from the Force.

1.

MAKING THE MAN:
LIFE BEFORE THE POLICE

Captain Athelstan Horn Popkess CBE, OStJ, KPM was born on 23rd November 1893 in the tiny settlement of Kynsnam, near to Bedford, in Cape Colony (now the Eastern Cape of South Africa) approximately 125 miles north east of Port Elizabeth, and grew up in the midst of the Boer War. Brother of Edmund, Ethelbert, Gilbert, Rosamund and Muriel, he was later quoted as saying that his "father favoured Saxon names".[4] It was a fairly privileged upbringing, typical of white people in colonial South Africa at the time, with an extended group of native servants including at least a cook, a nurse, a gardener and a coachman to wait on the family.

He spent his childhood growing up quickly in the plains of South Africa and later Southern Rhodesia, living a life very much akin to something from a Rudyard Kipling novel. Luckily, the adult Capt. Popkess, with his passion for writing and history, realised the uniqueness of his childhood and wrote the autobiography of his formative years *Sweat in my Eyes*, enabling a detailed insight into this extraordinary youth.

One outlandish example of this exceptional childhood is

4   *The Sun-Herald*, May 3rd 1959 pp.40

captured in one of his earliest memories, describing how on one occasion the neighbours' pet baboon picked up a nearby child and 'kidnapped' it up a tall tree, only being rescued by the quick intervention of its owner climbing after it and coaxing the child out of the baboon's arms.

Popkess quickly experienced the harsh realities of bush life in his frequent hunting trips and adventures with the other local boys. It is in fact almost miraculous that he lived to adulthood and could be said to have only narrowly cheated death on several occasions. In one awful incident, he was out dynamite fishing with some other boys when one of them neglected to throw the stick in time, blowing his hand off, bleeding to death in minutes and blinding another boy.

On another occasion one of his friends had managed to acquire a rifle and went out to go shooting with Popkess. Trying to get a bit of additional height, the boy climbed a pile of logs, but slipped:

> "To save himself from falling he pushed the carbine out behind him. There was a loud report. [We] saw that he was lying with his feet caught up on the top log. His head, or what was left of it, was resting on the ground. We fled."

In yet another similarly horrendous incident, Popkess narrowly cheated death whilst playing in a quiet stream with some friends, when he happened to get out to scoop some mud to throw at them. He tells of how he looked up stream and saw what "resembled a high wall, coming down the river at great speed". This 'great wall' was a freak surge of water; the result of a flash flood further upriver. Popkess shouted a warning to his two compatriots, who began climbing out just as the torrent struck. The previously serene stream became a thunderous raging deluge, and the young Athelstan's friends were lost to view. After Popkess ran to get help, an exhaustive search was conducted for the two boys by the townsfolk. It was only the following day after the raging waters had subsided that their lifeless bodies were found some five miles downstream, their arms locked desperately clinging to one another.

It was during this formative period of his youth that Popkess appears to have had his first encounter with 'the law', when bathing in a local pond with friends. This was forbidden at the time due to a drought, and the water needing to be kept for drinking. A policeman came along, discovering the boys, and Popkess narrowly avoided arrest by fleeing from the officer – naked from the waist down! He was chased through the town in that scantily-clad state by the officer, much to the amusement of the local villagers. In a bizarre serendipitous twist of events, he was to be reunited with this police officer many years later, during the First World War on a troop ship. Popkess, by this time a lieutenant, was approached by a sergeant who asked if Popkess recognised him. When informed that he didn't, the sergeant replied:

> "It was when you were a lad. Perhaps I shouldn't remind you of it now, Sir. You see, you were in your shirt only at the time; I was the policeman who chased you!"

In 1914 Popkess was out hunting lions with a friend (appropriately named Simba), camping for the night under a baobab tree. Another party of hunters had come across them and joined their camp. After some small talk, one of the newcomers told them there was a war on. "Who's in it?" asked Popkess, receiving the reply "Everybody! The Russians, the French, even the Belgiques! Germany started it." This obviously riled young

Athelstan, who "always reckoned that Kaiser was a wrong 'un," and that "them sort is always liable to start a war." So in his youthful exuberance, he decided to "give him and his Germans hell!"

He immediately went to the nearest township and from there headed to Salisbury, Rhodesia, where they were forming the Rhodesia Regiment for service in then German South-West Africa. Popkess had been in the Officer Training School whilst in school, which enabled him to enlist as an officer, leading his own Section. He was initially deployed to assist in quelling a Boer uprising, but saw no combat during it. He remained on garrison and guard duties whilst an elite hand-picked unit took on the rebel fighters.

On a later deployment, after landing from a transport ship into enemy territory Popkess' sense of morality was evident. As senior officer present he helped prevent the looting of an address in one of the towns they marched through, posting sentries throughout their stay to ensure it was not touched.

His first encounter with the enemy could easily have been his last, if they hadn't been as hapless as he was incompetent. It occurred one night when he had been posted as part of a two-man reconnaissance team in an outlying house that was being frequented by Germans overnight. He was hiding in an attic with his compatriot, and both men were unable to stay awake. Suddenly Popkess was awakened by the sound of German voices below. Attempting to gently rouse his colleague, he startled the slumbering private, who promptly put his leg through the ceiling of the room below, in which the Germans were sitting. Not having their kit to hand, the German soldiers high-tailed it out of the house, Popkess emptying the clip of his pistol after them, but not hitting a single one.

The young lieutenant and the private were left with red faces when their compatriots, on hearing the shooting, came to their assistance and asked what had occurred. There is no doubt that as Chief Constable, Popkess would most likely have had serious disciplinary concerns should one of his constables have been caught napping on duty; although perhaps he would have chuckled inwardly at the reminiscence of his own youth.

Another incident that raised discipline concerns in the young lieutenant occurred whilst he was supposedly on garrison duty at an outpost. Popkess took a group of native 'commandos' on a day-long mission without the knowledge of his superiors. Future Chief Constable Popkess may have balked at this 'off-piste' unplanned mission had it been conducted by one of his subordinates without his say-so. Conversely, though, he may have admired the initiative and drive demonstrated during a lack of other orders. It was an early demonstration of Popkess creating opportunities for himself and demonstrating ingenuity.

It was also around this time that he experienced his first aerial bombing and a display of aircraft capabilities at the hands of the sole German aircraft in South Africa, which had been there for an exhibition at the outbreak of war. A single bomb was dropped from this aircraft, on a colleague of the young lieutenant, although this does not appear to have exploded. He also experienced trained working dogs, which were sent to his unit to assist with outpost duties. Both of these must have made lasting impressions on the young lieutenant, as both the use of trained dogs as well as air raid prevention and precautions were to play key roles during his career in the police.

His first taste of battle was the major infantry engagement at Trekkopjes, during which he was shot in the leg. In a demonstration of his character, Lieutenant Popkess continued to engage the enemy, supporting a very small and weak flank against enemy aggression and appears to have barely noticed the wound that had gone clean through his calf. Not wanting to miss anything "just as things were likely to get more exciting," he concocted a poultice and stuffed it inside the wound. This initially worked well, but he was then sent on two marches that opened up the wound which subsequently became infected.

This attitude of carrying on in the face of adversity to see the job done was to become perhaps the strongest trait in his character in his later life. It would see him continue working through a period of almost certain clinical depression, and was probably the cause of his stubbornness in the 'Popkess Affair' period. As a result of his injuries Popkess was sent to a hospital ship for a period of treatment and recovery. His befriending of the ship's registrar who seemed to have a large store of cold ale, fresh fruit and half-bottle of wine every meal time appears to have meant his stay wasn't too onerous...

Whilst he was laid-up in hospital the fighting in south west Africa ended. In line with his already proven desire not to miss the action, Lieutenant Popkess caught the next mail steamer to England. As he arrived in London, the city had just experienced its first Zeppelin raid, and the ever-inquisitive Popkess made his way to see one of the unexploded bombs. The aerial bombing of civilians must have further compounded his concerns over air-raids that was again to prove crucial to his persona in later years.

After the majority of his recovery was complete he reported to the War Office, where he was commissioned into the North Staffordshire Regiment. He then spent three months training, and five months in the Reserve Battalion on Guernsey "interspersed with badminton, Bridge in the Mess and dances and concerts in the gymnasium." This bored Popkess, who had travelled half the world specifically to participate in the fighting. He apparently wrote so often to the War Office to get stuck into the action that he received orders to head back to German East Africa, escorting a group of reinforcements for the Legion of Frontiersmen.

He was initially posted as Provost Marshal at Kisumu, on Lake Victoria, in charge of a sergeant major and 20 native military police, although Popkess wrote that both he and his predecessor in the role never could discover exactly what it was that they should be doing there. Again, rapidly bored by this dreary posting, after only a month Popkess once more took the initiative and travelled to where the colonel of the Frontiersmen was spending a week's leave. Luckily for Popkess, a renowned game hunter was with the colonel who happened to know many of the same people as Popkess. This serendipitous, if slightly nepotistic meeting, meant that Popkess was vouched for, which secured the favour of the senior officer. The colonel immediately approved Popkess' transfer into the Legion of Frontiersmen.

The success of this uninvited direct approach to a senior figure almost certainly influenced Popkess' thought process later in his life, when he dropped in on the Home Secretary unannounced in an effort to secure his appointment as Chief Constable.

The Frontiersmen were an elite unit primarily comprised of South Africans of European descent, raised in that wilderness and toughened to its harsh and unpredictable nature. All the troops in the Legion were the very definition of 'hard men', with strong athletic builds and the mental fortitude to just 'get on with it' in that vast expanse of nature. Popkess praised his compatriot soldiers in that regiment highly, taking pains to describe their strength and abilities, and described how any joshing or ribbing usually ended up in an amicable bout of 'Queensbury rules' boxing; a feat at which Popkess claims he was also praised by his new peers.

He fought with this unit for three hard years before it was "so depleted and fever-stricken that, except in spirit, they ceased to be an effective unit in the field." They were evacuated to Cape Town to recuperate, but Popkess, again demonstrating that he was not one for idling, transferred to the King's African Rifles. During a short campaign enforcing a tactical German withdrawal, Popkess saw many of his subordinates and seniors killed in action. During various short postings across the region he still refused to idle, describing hunting excursions, including on one occasion shooting and killing a rhinoceros in just two very accurate well-placed shots. This was a time and location when the impact of such hunting was not known, and such actions were considered acts of great skill.

Popkess also describes leading tracking parties after roving bands of Germans who had ambushed a supply column, during which he again demonstrated his inspirational leadership by taking the vanguard of his scouting party. During this mission Popkess cheated death in almost Hollywood-esque fashion, when he stumbled unexpectedly across the German raiding party he was pursuing. Before he could realise he was knocked off his feet, having been shot in the chest. In what must be exceptionally long odds, the bullet struck a cartridge clip on the front of a shoulder strap for his backpack and did no more than badly bruise him!

Less than a month later, when returning to his base, again with some provisions, a German party ambushed them and took Popkess and his small group of soldiers and porters prisoner.

Using his cunning and guile, Popkess made some ruse to fetch items from his trunk, which had been dropped at the edge of where the group had settled for lunch. Sensing an opportunity, Popkess and his personal native servant made a break for it, the Germans shooting the fleeing Lieutenant's hat clean off his head. His servant however wasn't so lucky, getting shot in the back and dying instantly. Without weapon, food or water, Popkess fled through the jungle. Having narrowly escaped re-capture on one occasion when the German patrol passed within feet of him whilst he was taking water from a stream, two days after escaping his captors Lieutenant Popkess was found by an English patrol.

After being reunited with his unit, Popkess's commander was struck down with malaria and evacuated to hospital. This left Popkess in charge, when one evening he himself was under the grip of a fever, and heard a gunshot from one of his camp's outlying picquets. Lieutenant Popkess sent his new servant to investigate, and he returned with a private soldier who had inadvertently shot his own hand. Popkess looked at the injury and after assessing it writes that there "was only one thing I could do about the finger, and that was to cut it off... [because] the finger couldn't have been stuck on again by even the cleverest of surgeons." The young Lieutenant took his safety razor and cut off the soldier's finger himself. The company Sergeant-Major then obligingly emptied the cordite from a cartridge onto the wound and put a match to it, instantly cauterising it. To top off the poor private's misfortunes, in a demonstration of typical military black humour, Popkess then handed the severed finger back to the private telling him "there you are; it's yours."

It was after this that Popkess himself succumbed to his fevers, after his home-made remedy of a tonic of turpentine and water ceased to be effective. So determined was Popkess to remain with his unit at the Front that it was only after his stomach began to bleed, resulting in him regularly vomiting blood, a delirium setting in that made him walk off into the jungle on more than one occasion, and ultimately the loss of the use of his legs, that he was forcibly stretchered away by his troops. Upon his arrival at hospital, Popkess describes the pain from his stomach cramps as being so bad that "could I have laid my hands on a lethal weapon, I would have killed myself."

His illness was diagnosed as malaria, and to help the pain he was put on Morphia (morphine). This, coupled with the fever of the malaria, caused several days and nights of violent hallucinations, as a result of which he was tied to the bed. In one particularly bad hallucinogenic episode he broke free one of his arms and grabbed the medical orderly by the throat, and was only prevented from strangling him by the prompt intervention of other staff. The incident led to him being put in a straitjacket. His experience of being given this drug, coupled with his experience of dealing with it from a policing perspective later on, most likely contributed to him choosing to write one of his *Police Journal* articles on the subject, entitled 'Morphia the Slayer'.

Whilst recuperating some weeks later, Popkess bumped into his older brother 'Jim', neither of whom initially recognised one another after some 16 years apart, since he had run away from home aged 16 to join the army during the Boer War. Jim delivered Popkess the tragic news that another of their brothers, Ted – Edmund – had been killed fighting at Ypres in Flanders. Ted had been Popkess' closest brother in their youth, which made the news hard for him to take. To make this difficult period of his life even worse, a week or two after his encounter with his brother, after having been sent to an army convalescent retreat, he caught 'Blackwater', a particularly severe form of malaria from which

70% of sufferers died at the time. Once again Lieutenant Popkess was in and out of consciousness for weeks, and he describes how, after a period of time, he caught sight of himself in a mirror. He was horrified to see that his face had turned to the colour of mud (a common symptom of the illness), and that he looked severely emaciated.

Once partially recovered he was given six months' paid leave by the Army, which he was advised was to be spent in England. There, he reported to the Colonial Office doctor who was an expert on tropical diseases, who reported on him as being "unfit to return to the Tropics", and so Lieutenant Popkess was sent back to the Staffordshire Regiment, his six months' leave cancelled. As final icing on the cake of this disastrous period of his life, due to no longer being on service in the 'Tropics', his additional wage stipend was discontinued and he became overdrawn with the bank.

***

After the war, having just married his first wife Gilberta, a relationship which will be looked at in more detail in the chapter Preparedness, Popkess rejoined the North Staffordshire Regiment and served in Ireland during the Anglo-Irish War of 1919–21 as an "Intelligence Officer and Liaison with Royal Irish Constabulary".[5] During this period, he was to receive intelligence that a key Irish Republican Army figure would be travelling down a certain road. Popkess was reported to have lain in wait all night in a bush on the expected route, armed with a light machine gun, to pre-emptively kill his target.

---

5   The National Archives 45/24711 Application form for Chief Constable of Nottingham City Police Capt. Athelstan Popkess

Criminologist Dr Chris Williams tells how "It's a false alarm, but that's the kind of man he was. Throughout his life he is the sort of man who would get up at two in the morning to sit in a hedge and machine gun an IRA leader personally."[6]

After two years in the North Staffordshire Regiment Popkess was seconded to the Palestine Gendarmerie and Police for two years as Assistant Provost Marshal between 1922–24. After this two year secondment, he then returned to the North Staffordshires. On 8th March 1928 he was promoted to the rank of Captain, and on 15th May 1928 appointed as Assistant Provost Marshal, Aldershot Command.[7] Presumably this post came about from his experiences in Africa and the Palestine Gendarmerie as a provost. His actions when serving in Aldershot will be examined in more detail in the chapter Roads Policing, but it is sufficient to say here that his actions in this posting were perhaps key to his appointment to the Chief Constable position, as well as in developing his passion for Roads Policing and Traffic control.

In 1930, aged only 37, he was appointed as Chief Constable of Nottingham City Police. The influences of Popkess's early life and career can be clearly seen constantly resurfacing in his policies, endeavours and behaviours throughout his Police career. The attitudes learned from serving in the military, and most notably in the Legion of Frontiersmen where he fought alongside truly 'hard men', also echoed strongly in Popkess' police recruitment policies. So entrenched was his respect or deep-help faith in those who demonstrated a particularly notable physical presence, that this was to inspire some of his most notable recruits to the

6   www.bbc.co.uk/nottingham/contentarticles/2009/01/20/chief_constable_
    popkess_feature.shtml Nottingham's Famous Captain. Accessed 2017
7   London Gazette issue 33387, 25th May 1928 pp. 3654 and issue 33389, 1st June 1928
    pp. 3783

Nottingham City Police years later.

PCs Dennis 'Tug' Wilson RVM and Geoffrey Baker RVM had both been Grenadier Guards, acting in that capacity as pallbearers at the funeral of King George VI, and who stood at 6' 8½" and 6' 8" tall respectively. Such was their bearing and physical appearance that, following the funeral, both men were 'head-hunted', in today's parlance, by Capt Popkess to serve in the Nottingham City Police. Both were immediately posted almost permanently to the city's Old Market Square beat, on which, according to Bob Rosamund, an officer of the time, "only the very tallest could work". From this posting, both became local legends of their own, 'Tug' Wilson in particular, with his distinctive handlebar moustache. PC Rosamund tells us that even in general "only officers over 6'2" were allowed to work anywhere in the City Centre at all."

This policy was no doubt a result of the respect that Popkess had formed for 'tough men' during his childhood in South Africa and Rhodesia inspired by famous game hunters, and then his time with the Legion of Frontiersmen. It was also not necessarily a new concept in policing, especially in inner-cities, where the idea of a 'tough copper' was essential to dealing with those under-class of individuals intent on doing harm to others – especially police officers. In this period before radios, double-crewing and quick back-up, policemen (and it was mostly men) had to be tougher than those who sought to flee from them and would have no qualms about using violence in order to do so. Clearly Popkess felt that one easy way to quickly intimidate those persons was for the officers in those areas to have an imposing physical presence, immediately setting the ne'er-do-well on the back foot.[8]

8   Emsley, Clive: *The English and Violence since 1750* (Hambledon and London: London. 2005)

*Boxer Mohammed Ali tries to float like a butterfly
to the heights of Tug Wilson*

We can also see memories of his earlier life experiences in his attitude towards sports in police, most notably boxing. It has been demonstrated above that Popkess grew up in an environment when athleticism, strength and stamina could mean the difference between life and death. The abilities and strength of the Frontiersmen no doubt also demonstrated to him how it made those locals into an elite and specialist unit. This is almost certainly what drove Popkess to place such an onus on sporting prowess amongst his officers. Boxing for him perhaps demonstrated these skills more than any other, showing strength, stamina, physicality and mental fortitude. This is inevitably what led him to value that activity above all others, as shall be seen in the chapter Sports, on page 121.

2.

A CONTROVERSIAL CHOICE

It will become apparent that Capt Popkess was at times a very controversial figure. The issues surrounding him began even before the start of his tenure as Chief Constable of Nottingham City Police. His very appointment to the role was probably the most contentious issue of his police career, barring the incident that ended it – The Popkess Affair (see page 90). As stated previously, Popkess was a left-field candidate for the role of Nottingham City Police Chief Constable, whose appointment should almost certainly have never happened. To this day an element of mystery still remains around the full circumstances of how he succeeded in gaining the position.

With the retirement of the former Chief Constable Lt Col. Frank Brook in 1929, the Nottingham Watch Committee advertised for the upcoming vacancy. At the time, it was commonplace for external appointees with a 'suitable background' to take over stewardship of police forces. This was perhaps more common in 'County' forces than in City (Borough) forces, as the position of Chief Constable in County forces was seen as quite a respectable social position. County Chief Constables would be expected to 'hob-nob' with the local gentry, and attend formal society soirees. Chief Constables of urban forces, however, were expected to be more 'rough around the edges' and have a degree of understanding about policing, law and order, although a similar understanding about the command of a body of disciplined men was also acceptable.[9] This was confirmed by a Home Office document dated 1928, which stated that County Chief Constables were seen as 'higher functionaries of the county', whereas Borough Chief Constables were expected to have worked their way up through the ranks.[10]

In line with the above, the advert for the vacancy for the Chief Constable of Nottingham City Police stipulated a requirement for previous policing experience. From 38 applicants, a shortlist was drawn up and presented to the City's Watch Committee comprised of three candidates, all of whom were serving Chief Constables from smaller Borough forces of Derby, Maidstone and Swansea. Capt. Rawlings of Derby had in fact also been a police officer in the Nottingham City force before heading to Derbyshire, and initially appears to have been the favoured candidate. He certainly became so amongst Popkess' detractors after his appointment.[11] When the Watch Committee met on 20th November 1929 they adjourned, asking for the list to be increased to four. On 29th November 1929 the Committee reconvened, and it was this latecomer to the shortlist that was ultimately awarded the post of Chief Constable of Nottingham City Police. This person was Capt Popkess.

9   Cowley, Richard: *A History of the British Police: From its Earliest Beginnings to the Present Day* (Gloucestershire: The History Press 2011) p.67 and Wall, David: *The Chief Constables of England and Wales. The socio-legal history of a criminal justice elite* (Hampshire 1998) passim.
10 The National Archives (TNA): PRO, HO144/20637, Briefing Document 9 July 1928, D(b)-(c).
11 (TNA) PRO HO45/2471 'The Nottingham Chief Constableship' in *Police Review,* 7th December 1929

Some of the principal underlying reasons Popkess' appointment was so controversial from the outset stemmed from some key policies which existed at the time. Labour Party doctrine during this period specifically mandated against the appointment of army officers to public sector roles. Nottingham was at that time a Labour stronghold, and the bulk of the Watch Committee comprised of Labour councillors.

In addition to this, Regulation 9 of the *Police Regulations 1920* stated that no Chief Constable should be appointed who had no prior police experience unless they possessed some exceptional qualification or experience which specially fits them for the post.[12] Popkess had never previously served in a police force and came from a purely military background, so therefore on face value did not meet either of these criteria. He should by that reckoning never have made the shortlist at all.

The Watch Committee of Nottingham comprised Aldermen from all political parties in the Council, as well as lay members including Justices of the Peace (Magistrates). As such they were not directly controlled by the local Labour Party, who at that time held a significant majority on Nottingham City Council. The leader of the Watch Committee, Alderman Herbert Bowles, was, however, a Labour Party representative. Bizarrely, it appears it was Bowles who ultimately became the driving force behind Popkess' instatement, after initially opposing it. Indeed, it was he who, after initially rejecting Popkess for the shortlist, adjourned the meeting on 20th November for Popkess' name to be added.

The reasons for Popkess' choice remain unclear, and there appear to be no surviving minutes concerning the discussions that

---

12 Cowley: *A History of the British Police* pp. 152.

led to his appointment.[13] It seems probable that the Committee accepted that Popkess' roles as Assistant Provost Marshal from Aldershot, Palestine and South Africa constituted 'prior policing experience'. Indeed, the Town Clerk noted in his minutes book on 5th December 1929:

> "As regards service he has served for
>
> 2 years as intelligence officer in Ireland in close liaison with the R.I.C [Royal Irish Constabulary]
>
> 2 years in the Palestine Gendarmerie & police
>
> 1½ years as Provost-Marshal at Aldershot working in close co-operation with Hants and Berks police.
>
> Also for a period stated he has been attached to the Divisions of the Berks Police. He has good testimonials. This seems to me to make him a stronger case than Maj Clayton & whether or not this Palestine service is "previous police experience" I think he must be held to have "some exceptional qualification or experience which specially fits him for the post" for purpose of Regulation 9 & there is no case for turning down the local authority
>
> ? approve appointment". [14]

It's important to note here, however, that in another minor controversy, in Popkess' application form he describes himself as 'Provost Marshal' of Aldershot command – the man in charge, whereas in fact he was merely an Assistant Provost Marshal. This discrepancy was again cause for his detractors to raise issue with his appointment, with the *Police Review* of 20th December 1929

---

13 Bowley, Alfred S "Politicians and the Police in Nottingham: The Popkess Affair, 1959" in *Transactions of the Thoroton Society of Nottinghamshire Vol. 108* (2004) p. 175.

14 TNA: PRO HO 45/24711 Minutes of Nottingham Town Clerk, date stamp 5th December 1929.

highlighting this very issue as a cause for debate amongst the Nottingham City Council.

It may also be partly due to the fact that "during the inter-war period the Inspectors [of Constabulary] were showing increasing interest in some new issues, such as traffic management."[15] Popkess would certainly present an outstanding candidate if the Watch Committee were conscious of this focus by the Inspectorate, highlighted by the testimonials mentioned by the Town Clerk.

Alfred S Bowley, a former Chief Superintendent of Nottingham City Police turned historian, posits that Popkess' experience in controlling public unrest from his time working in military intelligence in Ireland in conjunction with the Royal Irish Constabulary was in fact the 'stand-out qualification' that best suited him for this post. Popkess' own application form for the job reads "2 years Intelligence Officer and Liaison with the Royal Irish Constabulary in Ireland", implying that not only did he liaise with the RIC as part of his army intelligence role, but that being the liaison officer actually *was* his role. He in fact lists this first in the 'Policing Experience' section, perhaps demonstrating that to him it was his most relevant policing experience. This role would have given him a great insight into dealing with large scale public unrest, and the inner workings and tactics of the police at the time through being involved in joint planning and strategy sessions.

He appears at great pains to stress this insight into civil police planning and tactics. Point 3 on his application form expands on the details about his close liaison with the local forces when

---

15 Emsley, Clive: *A Police Officer and a Gentleman: A.F 'Michael' Wilcox* (London: Blue Lamp Books 2018) p. 9.

working at Aldershot command. Here, he specifically highlights that he undertook an attachment with Berkshire Constabulary "to study Civil Police Administration and methods in England". [16]

His proven history of dealing with public unrest and violent dissidence in Ireland was perhaps of significant importance to the Watch Committee discussing the potential new Chief Constables. The vacancy arose at a time of great political unrest in the traditionally volatile working class city of Nottingham. The Wall Street Crash had occurred just one month prior to the advertising of the Chief Constable position, and the city's political elite perhaps feared uprisings and demonstrations by those affected. This may well have been an important consideration to the Watch Committee, and it is interesting to note that his "close liaison with the RIC" is specifically mentioned in the above quoted Town Clerk's minutes, alongside the fact that he was an army intelligence officer. The presumed assumption here is that the Watch Committee could infer from his experience that Popkess had the ability to gather information and act on it decisively in an effort to prevent larger unrest. This had been aptly demonstrated in the incident where he waited for the senior IRA figure in a hedge in order to execute him, as outlined in the chapter Making the Man; although the Watch Committee would have almost certainly not known about this specific incident.

After submitting his application to the Watch Committee and making the shortlist, there was quite a period of delay and concern around the potential appointment of Popkess. This arose from many people in positions of authority who felt that he *did* lack the relevant policing experience required under Regulation

---

16 TNA: PRO HO/24711 City of Nottingham, Appointment of Chief Constable, Form of Application: Captain Athelstan Popkess.

9. Indeed the City Council appear to have sent several fact-finding deputations to Aldershot to speak to Popkess' superior officers, the local police and council.

Popkess clearly caught wind of this, and decided to take his own action. From his experiences during his posting at Lake Victoria when he had visited the Colonel of the Frontiersmen and been drafted into that unit, and from his visit to the War Office whilst on recuperative duties in England, securing his posting back to South Africa, Popkess clearly believed in the direct approach. These previous examples had all worked in his favour. His desire to get the Nottingham City Police job became no exception.

To help smooth the process Popkess went directly to the Home Secretary, who would be the one to ultimately ratify any appointment. Arriving unannounced and without an appointment, luck again seems to have favoured The Captain, who was granted a meeting with the Secretary of State.

The Home Secretary of the time, John Clynes, noted that Popkess spoke with him about several deputations sent by Nottingham City Council to Aldershot barracks, and to ascertain "how he stood" with the Home Office. Clynes, however, felt that Popkess had another ulterior motive; "actually to try to 'work' the HO [Home Office]" to support his appointment. Once again, as with the Frontiersman colonel, Popkess seems to have known someone who knew the Home Secretary. This serendipitous nepotism again appeared to gain him favour, with Clynes noting in his same message "I have heard, too, from someone that knows his work well that he is a hard worker."[17] It is not clear who the intended addressee of this note was, but were it anyone

---

17 TNA: PRO HO 45/24711, Note from Home Secretary undated

associated with the appointment process, such praise from the Home Secretary cannot have hindered Popkess' cause. Once again, Popkess' direct approach appears to have borne fruit.

Given Popkess' single-minded determination to achieve his goals through making direct approaches to key individuals, it could also be possible to surmise that prior to the Watch Committee meeting on 20th November, he made some private communications with Alderman Bowles or the other members. This direct approach could be what caused them to radically change their positions. The *Police Review Journal* of 27th December 1929 indeed makes reference to a Town Council meeting in which Alderman Bowles alleged that all bar one of the candidates on the shortlist had canvassed members of the Watch Committee about their appointment. Such canvassing was in specific contravention of the job advertisement, and should have resulted in those candidates being disqualified.

Given Bowles' late day vociferous support of Popkess, it could be conversely argued that Popkess was the one candidate he believed had *not* canvassed the Watch Committee. Sadly there is no naming of the candidates allegedly involved in order to support or refute this.[18]

Upon hearing of the Watch Committee's decision to appoint Popkess, there began an immediate backlash against the new 'Chief-elect'. The Labour City Council passed a resolution that the Watch Committee should reconsider Popkess's appointment, as 'his experience and outlook' was "purely Military in character, and differing fundamentally from those demanded in the Civil Police." They also argued that it was "asking too much of the

18 *Police Review* 27th December 1929 clipping in TNA: PRO HO 45/24711

Nottingham citizen to accept as Chief Constable one of the Black and Tans [Royal Irish Constabulary]", who had caused great unrest in Ireland through excessive use of force, and were a key cause of the Irish uprising that had led to independence in 1921.

The local Labour Party also wrote to the Home Secretary seeking for him to annul Popkess' appointment, but just three weeks later the Home Secretary wrote back to the concerned Aldermen that it was not his place to override the decision of the local Watch Committee to install the person they felt best positioned to lead their force.[19] The resistance to the appointment did not stop there though, with non-local (Plymouth Devonport) MP Leslie Hore-Belisha even asking the Home Secretary questions about Popkess' suitability in Parliament.

It wasn't just the City Council who were opposed to Popkess' appointment. Both the Police Federation and the Superintendents' Association also made representations against it. Their issues also seemed largely based around Popkess lacking any civilian policing experience. They cited the generally held consensus that Borough force Chief Constables should by-and-large be appointed after having made their way up through the ranks as police officers, based on experience and merit. They published open letters in the *Police Review* highlighting that "such appointments as these are causing great dissatisfaction in the Police Forces of the Country".[20]

It would seem that their ire was not directed solely against Popkess, as in the case of the City Council, but more generally

---

19 TNA: PRO HO 45/24711, letter from Nottingham Labour Party to Home Secretary 7th December 1929 and letter from Home Secretary to Nottingham Labour Party 28th December 1929.
20 *Police Review*, 20th December 1929 and 27th December 1929.

against direct appointments to top policing positions, of which Popkess was merely the current example. This issue may, however, have been exacerbated in Popkess' case by his comparatively humble rank of Captain (only the second tier of commissioned officer, equivalent only to a police Chief inspector), as well as his relatively young age of 37. It may be that had his rank been higher, there would have been less resistance; or perhaps more, with the more senior ranks again typically filling the County Force positions.

A normal army Captain may only supervise 100 or so troops, and if this was simply the case with Popkess, the staff associations objections may have had merit. Popkess' work experience, however, had included organising the massive Aldershot Tattoos. This had demonstrated his ability to effectively organise, arrange and supervise large numbers of subordinates over a wide area. In fact, his application form specifically highlights this, saying "There are 42,000 troops and their families under my jurisdiction" under the 'Policing Experience' section. This may have been merely a sixth of the population of Nottingham at the time, but it probably did demonstrate to his supporters on the Watch Committee the level of responsibility he held for maintaining law and order over large populations.

None of the Council or Police organisations protestations bore fruit, however. The Council's appeal to the Home Secretary and his rejection of it was possibly the last throw of the dice. In early January of 1930, Capt Athelstan Popkess became the Chief Constable of Nottingham City Police. As a final mark of their disapproval, when the Watch Committee met on 8th January they formally recorded their appreciation for the outgoing Chief Constable, but no record of welcome is apparent for their incoming appointee.

His appointment was only to prove the first of many controversies that were to follow The Captain during his thirty-year spell as Chief Constable. It is these controversies to which the next chapter is devoted.

3.

CONTROVERSIES

Perhaps in response to his critics on the City Council and Superintendents' Association who had suggested that Popkess lacked police experience, within six months of his employment he appointed George Downs as his Deputy Chief Constable. Downs was a veteran police officer and a local one at that, having served in every rank in the Nottingham City Police, cutting his teeth in the city's slum districts. The appointment was ratified by the City's Watch Committee who, after the troublesome start that they had with Popkess, sought a counterbalance to his personality and leadership.

Former staff officer to Capt Popkess between 1953 and 1956 Chief Superintendent Dennis Silverwood (ret.) recalls how Downs was brought in primarily to take over discipline in the force, with Popkess being exceptionally regimented and even "ruthless" at the outset. Silverwood reminisces about how, especially in Popkess' early days, men were summarily dismissed for very minor infractions such as smoking on duty or even gossiping to the officer on the neighbouring beat area.

Former Policewoman Mary Needham can testify to this strict discipline, recalling a time as late into Popkess' stewardship as the mid-1950s, when she failed to salute the Policewoman

Chief Inspector on entering a room. As a result she was promptly issued an appointment to see the Chief Constable for a reprimand. Reporting in her full dress uniform, Popkess simply told the young-in-service policewoman, "If you do not alter your ways you can go and exploit your talents elsewhere." In another incident, PW Needham was removed from duty on a Royal Visit to the City for allowing her ears to protrude out too much from under her hat![21]

When Downs came in he took over the discipline role amongst others, ensuring that officers could hope for slightly longer careers by bringing a slightly more tolerant and understanding approach to the process. As time progressed and The Captain's recruitment policies of actively favouring and even head-hunting ex-military personnel bore fruit, it meant that his standards came down a little (vicariously through Downs), and that the officers' standards similarly went up, coming as they did from a more regimented discipline background.

The pairing of Downs and Popkess proved to be exceptionally harmonious, and with Downs's wealth of experience Popkess left him to largely deal with the policing affairs of the force. Downs was essentially the operational Chief Constable in all but name. This allowed Popkess to devote his time and energies to all his projects and initiatives that led to Nottingham City Police being at the forefront of policing throughout the middle of the Twentieth century as will be seen in the chapter Innovations.

The isolation granted by Downs' running of the operational aspects of the force also allowed Popkess a lot of time to indulge anything he wanted. Whilst this time was by-and-large put to

21 Phillips, Robert & Andrews, Tom: *100 Years of Women in Policing Nottingham*: Nottinghamshire Police (2015) p. 26

Dennis Silverwood

good use through his innovating new policing methods and writing them up for the *Police Journal* or one of his published books, occasionally his work time was used for 'extra-curricular' activities.

In a bizarre juxtaposition to the strict disciplinarian and workaholic nature that he outwardly projected to his officers and the community, Popkess very much enjoyed writing children's stories. Under the pen name 'Bardo Kidogo' he penned stories about a tortoise called Tuk-Tuk. Dennis Silverwood recalls that Popkess could often be found in his office writing, but on more than one occasion he found The Captain writing one of his children's stories rather than policing matters!

It wasn't only DCC Downs that Popkess relied on to generate

the extra time during work hours that he needed to indulge his own interests rather than conduct the daily running of the Force. Dennis Silverwood recollects how during his time as Popkess' staff officer he would find it a lot easier just to reply to incoming letters on the Chief's behalf. Initially he said he would open the letters and either write the replies that Popkess dictated to him, or just leave the letters with the Chief Constable to reply to. But as time went on he began replying to the letters himself, and simply left them on The Captain's desk to sign – which he normally did without reading them. He apparently started doing this because he found it very difficult to read Popkess' handwriting. This was normally written in green ink, which was Popkess' hallmark, and also required PC Silverwood to purchase a magnifying glass in order to try and make sense of the Chief's scrawl.

This initiative did lead to one embarrassing situation when Silverwood opened a letter that transpired to be from Popkess' first wife, asking him to "pay up you old bugger" for some monies he presumably owed to her! Silverwood promptly put it straight back in the envelope and left it on his boss's desk...

***

Things were not all harmonious between The Captain's appointment and his retirement, and there proved to be several very public controversial episodes during his tenure as Chief. Perhaps the greatest of these was related to his passion for sport, and boxing in particular. His desire for his officers to have sporting prowess will be seen in the chapter Sports, but this led to an incident that obtained some minor infamy, and made the national news in 1936.

From early on in his time in command, Popkess had fostered

an amicable rivalry with other police boxing teams in Germany. As part of this, the Nottingham City Police boxing team went on an annual trip to Germany to challenge local police teams and German professional boxers. Unfortunately, political events in Germany in the 1930s were becoming increasingly worrisome following the Nazi Party's rise to power in 1933. In spite of this, Popkess continued to lead his men on their annual pilgrimage. As the politics in Germany became more extreme, he was keen to ensure that his trips became a beacon of friendship and diplomacy in an effort to maintain some level of peace and understanding between the two increasingly hostile nations. In one demonstration of this friendship, in 1935 when the boxing team were in Ulm, a painting was presented to them by the local police force there in honour of their visit and continued friendship. This is still owned by the force today.

In 1936 the boxing team visited Stuttgart and had an evening of boxing against the local force in front of a capacity crowd. What made this specific event memorable was the Nazi salute given by Popkess whilst giving an address in the ring, which was caught on camera. If viewed on its own and out of contemporary context, this could be hugely contentious, but it needs to be seen alongside the Berlin Olympics of the same year, in which athletes from all countries (barring Great Britain and USA) gave Nazi salutes to Hitler in the opening ceremony. The Nottingham City Police boxers and the Chief Constable also posed for pictures with their opponents and local officials, whom by that time were all wearing Nazi uniforms.

On a reciprocal visit by the Stuttgart team to Nottingham a year later, the visitors stayed at the County Hotel in Nottingham, next to the Theatre Royal and only a stone's throw from the City Police Headquarters. In honour of their guests the County Hotel flew a

Top: Popkess gives a Nazi salute in 1936
Bottom: Officers of the Stuttgart boxing team give
the salute at the statue to Albert Ball VC

Nazi Swastika flag alongside a Union flag, perhaps the only time such a juxtaposition occurred on the UK mainland.[22]

Sadly, no photograph seems to exist of this event; its significance in history almost certainly not being realised at the time. What *was* captured for posterity, however, was when the Stuttgart officers visited Nottingham Castle and, as a mark of respect, gave Nazi salutes at the statue of Nottingham's First World War Victoria Cross hero, Lt Albert Ball VC. Whilst the symbolism of the Nazi salute may now taint the image, it is notable for the respect shown by the German officers to a former enemy combatant honoured for his bravery in fighting their countrymen.

These images, of the force in Stuttgart and the German officers in Nottingham, are perhaps the only instances of British Police Officers from the mainland UK standing next to uniformed Nazis.

It was his decision to give the Nazi salute in Stuttgart, however, that gained Popkess his small measure of notoriety at the time. As will be seen in the chapter Preparedness, Popkess did not let his relationship with the Germans blind him to their foreign policy and world affairs. In fact, his visits and the additional knowledge gleaned from them may have gained him insight into the true state of affairs under Adolf Hitler, which enabled him to be so well prepared in terms of civil defence at the outbreak of the Second World War.

***

Views expressed by Popkess at the end of his career were also to prove controversial. On Saturday, 23rd August 1958, in

22 Hyndman, PC David: *Nottingham City Police: A Pictorial History 1930–1960* Newark: Davage Printing Ltd pp. 11

*Popkess and the Nottingham City Police boxers
pose with their opponents and local officials*

what was to be the final full year of his tenure, rioting broke out on the St Ann's Well Road and wider St Ann's area of the city. The violence reportedly started after a West Indian man was seen dining with a white blonde-haired English woman. Racial tensions in the area and further afield at the time were high, and it appears that a couple of locals disapproved of the interracial couple and set about the young man.

Reports state that over one thousand people gathered in the area and the tension spilled over into running battles between groups, supposedly along racial lines. Dozens of people received injuries from knife wounds and bottlings. One police officer was even run over by a black male driver, who was latterly cleared by police of any charges. A senior officer was quoted as saying, "As far as we can make out, the driver was so scared that he dare not stop his car, thinking he might be lynched. So he just kept going."[23]

The clashes were almost universally labelled as 'race riots', with Nottingham's *Evening Post* of Monday, 25th August leading with the headline "Nottingham Racial Clash – Probe Goes On." The same paper quoted Lt Col John Cordeaux, MP for Central Nottingham, as saying:

> "Whatever the origin of this shocking business may have been, there is no doubt that it developed into a racial battle."

The Nottingham events sparked identically-motivated but much larger, more widely-reported rioting in London a week later.

Chief Constable Popkess was very vocal with his counter-

---

23 *Nottingham Evening Post*, 25th August 1958 p.1

opinion, stating repeatedly that the trouble was in fact as a result of "local hooligans", and was not racially-motivated. His argument ran that the violence was not racial because, as he stated in a press conference, "The coloured people behaved in an exemplary way by keeping out of the way. Indeed they were an example to some of the rougher elements."[24] This statement implied that disorder could only be racial in nature if caused by people of minority ethnicities, and doesn't take into consideration that the violence could have sprung up due to tensions between the white and black communities.

This opinion that the disorder was not racially motivated was not widely shared, and Popkess failed to convince many with his statements. They may have partially been borne out though by the fact that a week later crowds gathered once more in St Ann's, but this time the almost exclusively white crowd turned on itself. That event was lost in the news, however, due to the headlines being taken over by the Notting Hill rioting that had since broken out.

Popkess' statements perhaps even caused a worsening of community relations between the police and the black community. One modern article on the events on a black history website refers to his comments as "ignorant".[25] Perhaps by today's standards they are, but it is the job of today's observer to judge characters in history by the standards at the time. Given The Captain's background from Apartheid South Africa, coupled with British society at the time in the context of the Windrush era, 'ignorant' is perhaps too strong a word, and 'blinkered' or

---

24 Withers, Bill *Nottinghamshire Constabulary: 150 Years in Photographs* (Huddersfield: Quorn Publishing Ltd) p.22
25 www.blackpast.org/gah/nottingham-riots-1958 as accessed January 2017

'wishful thinking' may be more suitable.

In support of this, the same headline from the *Nottingham Evening Post* labelling the incident as a "race riot" continues with the sub heading "Police Vigil on Rest of City's Coloured Colonies". The choice of language here would make a modern reader cringe, but demonstrates the mindset of the time and how Popkess should not be singled out as abnormal by modern observers.

It is possible to hypothesise that Popkess was aware that he was to retire soon and wanted to protect his 29 year legacy. He would certainly not have wanted it to end with high-profile rioting over race issues that he perhaps felt could or should have been picked up in advance and nipped in the bud by his force. Certainly, members of the black community recall name-calling and having bricks thrown at their windows being common at the time, and this trend should have probably been identified by the City Police.[26]

Popkess may also have wanted to placate and appease the City Council regarding the event, trying to portray and maintain a positive image of the city, and not one with a significant racial and socio-economic divide. His childhood and early adult experiences regarding the extremes of segregation and treatment of the black population in South Africa also possibly had a bearing on his views of what constituted racial divide and tension, with this incident and the background to it falling far short of the racial issues prevalent in South Africa at this time. In any event, no matter what his motives in doing so, Popkess was almost alone in swimming against the popular tide regarding the circumstances of the riots.

26 news.bbc.co.uk/1/hi/uk/6675793.stm as accessed January 2017

The 'Nottingham Race Riots' were to be the first blow of Popkess' *Annus Horribilis* of 1958/59, and his statements regarding the riots possibly undermined some of his respect and popular support.

It may be, however, that in 1958 Popkess was suffering from what today would be diagnosed as depression. His second wife, Dorothy, to whom he had been married since 1939, had committed suicide in 1956 aged 50, at their home at 35 Newcastle Drive on Nottingham's The Park Estate. On the afternoon of 23rd February that year she was found dead in the greenhouse by her stepdaughter Virginia, from Athelstan's first marriage, having taken an overdose of barbiturates. An inquest held on Monday, 27th concluded that Dorothy took her life because "the balance of her mind was disturbed by ill-health" after she had been "suffering from nervous depressions and obsessions". The inquest heard from Virginia that Dorothy had had a breakdown just before Christmas the preceding year, and her physician, Dr Jaffé, testified that he had been treating her for that ailment since New Year's Eve, but that Dorothy had told him she did not feel the treatment was working.[27]

Dorothy had clearly been Athelstan's rock during their marriage, and the *Nottingham Evening Post* of the following day recorded how she often attended formal functions alongside the Chief Constable. Such was her influence among the local legal profession that the Guildhall Magistrates' Court stood for a moment's silence the following morning, led by the city's Chief Magistrate.[28]

For a man who stood so alone in his work environment, it

27 *Nottingham Evening Post*, 27th February 1956 p. 5
28 *Nottingham Evening Post*, 24th February 1956 p. 9

can only be assumed that his wife would have been a very close confidante to Popkess and an ear for his woes. The cause of her nervous depressions and obsessions is not known, but it cannot have been helped by the amount of time that Popkess spent at work away from her, coupled with the policing duties she was expected to conduct in the time she was with him. The pair also had no children together, which could either mean she was unable to conceive or one of the pair perhaps did not want more; Popkess already had two from his previous relationship, Virginia Cherrie and Richard Simon Popkess.

Dennis Silverwood recalls how, after the tragic loss of his wife, Popkess "took to his bed" and the general orders at the time were to leave him alone and not to visit. Silverwood defied those orders and went to visit his Chief Constable, going for leisurely walks around The Park Estate with him. He describes during this time Popkess as very introverted and far removed from his previously driven, extroverted nature.

Whilst depression as an ailment had been highlighted by Freud in the early 20th century, it was still not widely accepted, or at least admitted, particularly on the part of men at this time. Options with regards to it were also limited at that time, given that anti-depressant medication did not even come into existence until the 1970s.

Given Popkess' character it can only be assumed that he would not have admitted to suffering depression as a result of his wife's tragic death. It must almost certainly be the case that he would not have sought medical or psychological assistance regarding it either. He would have almost certainly 'put on a brave face' and continued with his life and work duties, believing in his own mind that he should not show such a 'weakness' to his officers, partner agencies or the public, and probably feared that it would undermine his credibility and perceived ability to run the force.

If it is the case that Popkess suffered from depression – and from the account of Dennis Silverwood, it can be fairly assumed that he did – then this could explain why his last couple of years at the helm of Nottingham City Police were set so significantly apart from all the other years of his tenure.

Both the 'Race riots' and the 'Popkess Affair' occurred following the death of his second wife, when Popkess was almost certainly suffering from clinical depression, compounded by his feeling forced to hide it. This can easily explain why The Captain's normal composed and masterful leadership style was apparently lacking in the penultimate years of his command. Anyone who has suffered from or been close to someone suffering depression will testify how radically it can alter a personality – making the afflicted person terse, morose, short-tempered, introverted and belligerent. This matches Popkess' stubborn approach when refusing to accept that the St Ann's riots were racially motivated, and also why he persisted with his investigation into the City Council in the Popkess Affair in the face of such adversity. He would have refused to back down or accept that he could have been mistaken, because his depression was clouding his decision making and he was determined not to show his perceived weakness.

It is possibly the greatest tragedy of Popkess' career that after his incredible thirty years of policing service at the forefront of technological and policing policy development, the twilight of his career should be marred by this depression, which in turn probably led to him being at the centre of one of the greatest controversies in 20th century policing, an incident on a national scale with far-reaching implications. The significance and complexity of the Popkess Affair will be examined later in a chapter of its own.

4.

ROADS POLICING

It is not the controversies in which he became embroiled that make Popkess arguably the greatest police officer of the Twentieth century. It was his plethora of reforms and innovations that form the basis for this accolade. Perhaps one subject was a passion to Chief Constable Capt. Athelstan Popkess to innovate in above all others, and that was roads policing. He published books on the subject; developed whole new working methods around it (see chapter The Mechanized Division, page 84); gave lectures to the Royal Society for the Prevention of Accidents (RoSPA) and the Association of Chief Police Officers (ACPO) among others; and was ultimately inducted as an officer of the Knightly Order of St John (OStJ) in July 1959 for his influential work to reduce deaths and injuries on the roads during his term as Chief Constable of Nottingham City.[29]

It is to this passion that this chapter is devoted, looking at the myriad ways in which Capt. Popkess influenced and changed not only how the roads were policed, but also about how traffic flow was increased and most importantly ensured fewer people lost their lives to motor cars.

29 *The London Gazette* Issue 41764 14th July 1959 p. 4469

Popkess was Chief Constable through the period when motor cars changed from being an expensive luxury to an increasingly every day household essential. World War II brought huge leaps forward in the mechanisation of the whole country, and army surplus vehicles sold off after the war greatly increased the heavy goods traffic on the roads. It was also only at the very end of Popkess' tenure which saw the construction of the country's first motorway, all traffic until this time being in cities or 'country lanes'. This exponential rise in the use of motor vehicles caused a similar exponential increase in deaths and serious injuries as a result of road traffic collisions.

Figures quoted by Popkess in a paper he gave to a meeting of ACPO on 28th May 1957 make for stark reading:

"Up to December, 1944, 370,000 British people were killed and injured on all fronts in the last war. During the same period 588,000 people were killed or injured on our roads in motoring accidents. Do you know that in the 10 years before World War No. 2, motor vehicles maimed or killed more than two million people on the roads of Great Britain?"[30]

These are staggering figures given the comparatively low number of motor vehicles on the roads, especially during the Second World War at a time of fuel rationing. Compare this to official government figures from 2015, which show that there were 186,189 people killed or injured on the roads for the whole year – given the exponential rise since that time in the number

---

30 "Our Mounting Traffic Problems" Transcript of speech given to Association of Chief Police Officers Annual General Meeting 28th May 1957 available at www.open.ac.uk/Arts/history-from-police-archives/PolCit/resources/Guide.pdf pp. 152–159.

of cars, and an additional population of around twenty million.[31]

Popkess was keen to try and improve this situation, not solely due to the loss of life and injuries to persons, but also in the cost to the police of time and resources. In his same ACPO speech, Popkess quotes the Minister for Transport as saying the cost to the government nationally of road accidents at the time was £10m – roughly £1.7bn today. He further ventured at a RoSPA conference on 7th October 1959 that "accidents were costing infinitely more in life and property than crime."[32]

In both human and financial costs, therefore, Capt. Popkess was keen to reduce the number of road accidents both in Nottingham and further afield. To do so, he was keen to learn the causes of accidents in order to try and prevent them from occurring at all. He sought to do this by using a mixture of constructive, prohibitive and punitive measures.

In 1951 he published his book *Traffic Control and Road Accident Prevention*. This was a really ground-breaking work, which espoused many of the ideas and initiatives devised by Popkess during his tenure as Chief Constable and before. His experience organising the giant Aldershot Military Tattoos and more specifically the traffic control around them was most likely what initially lit the flame of passion for this book. The finished work is the result of the intervening 22 years' worth of research and study.

It explores every angle of the two aspects the title suggests, from various means of how to reduce accidents in terms of both

---

31 Reported road casualties Great Britain: 2015 annual report The Department for Transport www.gov.uk/government/uploads/system/uploads/attachment_data/file/556396/rrcgb2015-01.pdf
32 *Commercial Motor*, 9th October 1959 pp. 42

vehicle occupant and pedestrian casualties; addressing driver behaviours; the proper investigation of road accidents by police; and educating children, as well as how to increase traffic flow and ease congestion and everything else in between. He outlines how *Road Accident Prevention* is closely aligned with *Traffic Control*, be that by preventing pedestrians having to cross from behind parked cars or, in a sign of the times, outlining how coal deposited at the side of the road could be a hazard to cyclists.

One of the first things addressed by Capt. Popkess in the book is the issue of drinking and driving. He revisited this topic in an article entitled "The Drunken Driver" which was published in the *Police Journal* in 1956. 'Drink-driving' was not a new issue, and indeed the link between intoxication and driver impairment was well known. The Criminal Justice Act 1925 had first made it illegal to be drunk in charge of any mechanically-propelled vehicle, and the Road Traffic Act 1930 made it an offence to drive, attempt to drive or be in charge of a motor vehicle on a road or any other public place while being "under the influence of drink or a drug to such an extent as to be incapable of having proper control of the vehicle."

Popkess eloquently highlighted the issues with this legislation in *Traffic Control*, however. He tells of the "sobering up" effect of an accident or arrest by police, and the delay in then seeing a medical professional to ascertain drunkenness or intoxication. He cited a case where one doctor stated a male was unfit to drive but a second disagreed, meaning the case was thrown out in court. Popkess therefore wrote in favour of adopting a pioneering new American technology: specific scientific apparatus that can establish the level of alcohol in breath, blood or urine. He had clearly both done his research on the equipment and understood the science behind it, as he was able to explain its workings in the book. It is also clear that his belief in the equipment was such that he instructed the Nottingham City Police Forensic Laboratory to experiment with it and investigate the science themselves.

It appears that Nottingham City Police used the science as supporting evidence in drink-driving cases, significantly before legislation relating to specific alcohol limits. Popkess wrote about one example of a case in Gainsborough as early as 1947, where the Nottingham City Police labs tested a sample of blood and measured an alcohol level of 0.25%. In court the head of the laboratory cited research that conclusively showed that the blood alcohol level at which most people became significantly impaired was 0.08%, which is still the legal limit of alcohol in blood today. This evidence was able to be used in court to demonstrate the level of intoxication of the offender to show that they were indeed drunk, and not suffering from any other medical condition.

Traffic Control was published in 1951, and the above example given by Popkess dates from 1947. He was to further expound on his ideas in a paper published in trade journal *The Police Journal: Theory, Practice and Principles* in 1956, in a paper entitled "The Drunken Driver". In this article he re-iterated many of his points from *Traffic Control* but in a more succinct way, and incorporated even more of the latest research into the subject. He cited a recent report by the British Medical Association which had demonstrated from medical experimentation that the more alcohol people have in their body the less able they are to perform various simple actions, but that this level varies from person to person depending on their drinking habits. It then goes on to highlight how at a "certain concentration in the tissues, signs of intoxication sufficient to render it an offence to be in control of a vehicle will become evident in anyone, irrespective of his degree of 'tolerance'."

Popkess then goes on to examine a paper in the *British Medical Journal* from 1951 about the Danish experience of bringing in a specific drink-drive limit of µg of alcohol per 100ml of blood (and equivalent in urine). Popkess wrote how the study noted that accident rates due to alcohol fell from 10% to 2% following it being made compulsory for all drivers suspected of being in drink at the time of a collision to provide a blood sample.

In 'The Drunken Driver' and *Traffic Control*, Popkess took great pains to not only offer his solutions, but also to highlight what he felt were the key failings, and areas where legislation and the judicial system fell short, in order to justify why his initiatives were needed. In both works he quoted statistics around the issue of prosecuting those drivers suspected of being inebriated, without the assistance of a statutory limit of blood alcohol. He quoted Nottingham's accident statistics of the times at which road accidents occurred in 'The Drunken Driver'. These demonstrated that collisions peaked between 10.00 and 11.00pm – the time people would be driving home from the pub.

He also related how those drivers accused of drink-driving who appeared before magistrates would be convicted on the evidence of police officers and a police surgeon in 91% of cases. Conversely, however, those who took the case to Crown Court were only convicted in 52% of cases. Popkess suspected that this was to do with the jury sympathising with the accused motorist, speculating that perhaps some of those jury members too would have driven home on occasion after several drinks and not thought anything of it.

Perhaps most shockingly from today's standpoint, he also outlined how, at that time, prior to it being a legal requirement to provide a blood sample, any examination by a police surgeon could only be undertaken with the accused person's consent. Without that consent, the conducting of such an examination would be a criminal assault!

In 'The Drunken Driver' Popkess included a copy of the Nottingham City Police standing order in relation to dealing with those arrested on suspicion of drink-driving. It detailed exactly what to do and how to deal with any refusal to allow an examination. This is typical of The Captain when publishing his articles. He was not one to simply propose new solutions and leave it for the government to ponder and perhaps introduce at a later stage. Popkess was a man of action as well as thought, with all his initiatives and ideas introduced and tested in a live working environment in Nottingham, with the assistance of his City Police officers. This is evident in the above-mentioned drink-drive case from 1947, and shall be clear throughout this book with many other examples.

Specific limits of alcohol in the blood, urine and breath for drivers were not introduced in law until the Road Safety Act 1967 – some 20 years later. The Road Traffic Act 1962 had made mention of using scientific tests to help the police prove drunkenness, but fell short of setting actual limits.

This 20-year delay in introducing national legislation shows just how far ahead of his time Capt. Popkess was in this respect. The delay in introducing legislated limits came out of a general public outcry against its introduction. This opposition was based on both the fact that the 'offender' was not able to know at what point they had crossed the limit, and a general feeling that the test infringed on people's liberty – a non-consensual medical examination having previously been classed as a criminal assault.

His massive research towards the introduction of this legislation is perhaps one of Popkess' greatest contributions to policing and British society as a whole, having unquestionably saved countless lives since its introduction. Because he was so significantly ahead of his time with it, however, he has been robbed of any credit, and as with so many of his other innovations, his contribution has been largely lost to history. The same was also to happen with several of his other initiatives which would not see their introduction until after his time in office; especially in the field of roads policing.

***

Traffic Control went on to detail in great depth research and trials into a plethora of things to help reduce road casualties. Some 20 pages are devoted to street lighting; the various types available, spacing, positioning on bends and hills, brightness, dazzle in wet conditions, and changes dependent on road category all feature, along with pictures and diagrams to support his points. This in-depth research of a subject was so important to Popkess, as he always sought to be able to understand why and how things occurred, specifically in this case road accidents.

In *Traffic Control*, Popkess devoted numerous pages to detailing how police and other agencies should record traffic collisions. In what would now be familiar to any current or former police officer, local authority road planner or car insurance underwriter, Popkess expounded the virtue of 'accident cards'. These were documents to be completed by police officers attending the scene of traffic collisions, detailing routine facts such as details of the vehicles and persons involved, time of day and weather, as well as a brief outline of the circumstances.

Crucially, Popkess sought to go further than these basics. He argued that police should analyse the data from crashes based on a series of 'cause codes' outlined by the Ministry of Transport, based on what the attending officers considered to be the causes of the collision. He argued that it was the job of the police to look at trends in the causes of accidents in specific areas, and adapt patrol and enforcement strategies to reduce the risks.

These 'cause codes' could highlight existing or emerging trends in the reasons behind collisions and be put into easily-interpreted tables or graphs. The most frequent causes behind accidents in any given area could be pro-actively targeted by officers in an effort to reduce casualties. To this day, this gathering of accident data is a significant role of the police, using exactly the same methods. Today, the results are shared with local and national authorities to work on road improvements at 'accident blackspots', or to adjust speed limits etc – something Popkess would no doubt wholeheartedly approve of. These accident statistics have also given rise to campaigns such as 'The Fatal Four', whereby the leading four contributory factors in fatal accidents (speeding, drink driving, using a mobile phone and not wearing a seatbelt) are pro-actively enforced by police. This can be seen as a direct output of Popkess' desire to better understand and reduce the causes of accidents.

Many of the subjects on which Popkess wrote in *Traffic Control* were not new or innovative, such as accident recording or the study regarding street lighting. As Popkess outlined in his introduction to the work, however, they had not been compiled into one comprehensive volume prior to his. His stated intention was to collate the various research and theories from both the UK and abroad relating to his subject matter and compile them into a thorough and cohesive work. The same was true of his articles, and his citation of an essay in "The Drunken Driver" from the *British Medical Journal* shows that his research around his subject matter was extensive and varied – not simply being limited to policing publications.

Scattered throughout his works, though, are plenty of his own innovations, which are expertly interwoven with the academic and scientific theories and studies, the conclusions of which are used to support, justify and explain his own.

One example of this use of academic research is regarding tests for drivers. A compulsory driving test had been introduced in the UK with the Road Traffic Act 1934, but this was fairly basic. In *Traffic Control*, Popkess investigated ways to tell how 'accident-prone' people are, and how to improve those drivers and reduce their risk. He cited a study conducted on London bus drivers, which identified that a certain small percentage of the subject group were more than two times more likely to have accidents than their peers. He then discussed the various reasons why this might be so, and offered ideas how to improve their abilities; and by extension the abilities of the whole population.

His solutions, which he compiled from various sources and studies into driver improvement, comprise a variety of classroom-based tests that he argued should form part of any test for new drivers. Notably amongst these propositions is a 'reaction time' test, in which he suggests lights appearing on a screen and the prospective driver having to press a corresponding button. Another solution he offered is a test to measure a person's judgement of relative speeds. In yet another example of how far ahead of his time Popkess was, such ideas were not taken up in Britain until the introduction of the 'Hazard Perception Test' in 2002 – over fifty years after *Traffic Control* was published and long after Popkess' death.

Popkess also proposed a series of questions which would test a driver's knowledge regarding all aspects of driving and road safety. He even set an example 50 questions complete with answers. and proposed a pass mark of 35. A driving theory test along almost these exact lines was not introduced in the UK until 1996, 45 years after Popkess wrote his book.

Furthermore, his conclusions from the study of the London bus drivers also includes a suggestion for additional training of drivers who are more found to be more accident-prone. This could be seen as a foundation of the driver improvement courses offered as an alternative to prosecution to modern drivers caught speeding, driving carelessly or various other minor road traffic offences.

***

Popkess was not limited to what would now be seen as the 'policing' of the roads and driver standards, but was also one of the first to examine how to improve traffic flow and movement – an undertaking more commonly conducted presently by local authorities. As the title of the book would suggest, traffic control and flow was just as important to Popkess as police enforcement, which almost certainly grew out of his experience organising the Aldershot Military Tattoo.

This event, or more specifically Popkess' role in it, was best described by the commanding General of Aldershot when writing Popkess' reference on his application to Nottingham City Police:

> "This entails the regulation of a crowd of some 80,000 spectators and 5,000 performers with the concentration of up to 10,000 vehicles of all kinds on one night".

He continued in this glowing reference that he considered that Popkess "carried out this work in an exceptionally efficient manner, and shewed [sic] marked powers of organisation."[33]

In fact, this testimonial to Popkess' organisation of the Tattoos extends to approximately a third to a half of his reference from the commanding generals of Aldershot in support of his application to the Chief Constable position. Popkess was right to be proud, if he does not exaggerate in his application form for the Chief Constable position when he details how

> "the marshalling and control of traffic for the Tattoo started from a radial line 30 miles from Aldershot, and all traffic instructions for both the Civil Police ... and the Corps of Military Police were worked out in detail by me and issued ... from my office."

His pride is justified by the glowing and ubiquitous praise in the print media of the time, with the *Daily Mirror* writing under the headline 'Traffic Marvels of the Great Tattoo':

> "To me the feature of the great Searchlight Tattoo at Aldershot is the amazingly efficient organisation which extends for miles around the actual display... the huge car parks and the footways to the arena, cover an enormous space and are controlled by the co-operation of Police Civil and Military... with a skill that creates simple order where there would otherwise be chaos."[34]

The *Daily Mail* went even further in its praise for Popkess,

---

33 The National Archives (TNA): PRO, HO144/24711 Testimonial No.1 Major-General J. C Harding Newman & Lieutenant General G. M. Campbell from City of Nottingham Appointment of Chief Constable Form of Application Capt Athelstan Popkess
34 *Daily Mirror*, 20th June 1929 'Traffic Marvels of the Great Tattoo'

stating:

> "A detached observer at the scene of the Tattoo must have
> marvelled as much at the spectacle provided by the assembling
> as of the great show itself. Both are magnificently impressive;
> both are wonders of organisation... The condensing of tens of
> thousands of people on the Tattoo front is carried out with
> precision. Yet there is no confusion; the mighty throngs fit into
> their positions with the ease of an ordinary audience filling a
> theatre... [at the conclusion] thousands of motors glide away
> in all directions, as easily as they arrive."[35]

These are but two examples from around half a dozen in various
papers that week, which are reproduced in Appendix 1.

In an event comprising thousands of performers displaying
polished parade drill, feats of skill and showmanship and
immaculately turned out uniforms, for the traffic management
to be highlighted in such exultant tones by reviewers really
speaks volumes of Popkess' organisation skills. Clearly it stood
well beyond the standard practice of the time, once again
demonstrating Popkess as having been significantly ahead of his
contemporaries and standard processes at the time. In fact, he
used two whole typed pages of his application form for the Chief
Constable position to quote these press reports of the planning
of the Tattoo as 'policing experience', perhaps demonstrating his
pride at such glowing praise, in addition to another half a page of
his explaining his role as quoted above.[36]

Most likely having been encouraged and proven in his abilities

---

35 *Daily Mail*, 21st June 1929 'Tattoo Crows; Impressive System of Marshalling; Traffic
     without a Block'
36 TNA: PRO, HO144/24711 City of Nottingham, Appointment of Chief Constable,
     Form of Application, Captain Athelstan Popkess additional page 'Police Experience'

by this success and the glowing praise he received in the Press, *Traffic Control* details how traffic management plans should be produced for large public events. These plans, he stated, should detail all aspects of the region around the site including potential bottlenecks, crossings and road layouts, whilst also factoring in potential volume of traffic etc. He also stipulated that these plans should be updated following the event and kept for future reference in subsequent years. Clearly this was all informed from his first-hand experience with the Tattoos.

In addition to these fixed events, Popkess advocated the preparation of various emergency contingency plans in the event that certain major roads are closed. At the time of his writing, the police bore responsibility for all such traffic plans, whereas today these responsibilities fall on local authorities. Nonetheless, these ideas are prevalent throughout today's public and private sectors, with all police forces and local authorities having emergency and/or events planning departments, whose sole task it is to plan for such scenarios. Whilst it is not easy to say specifically when such departments were first set up, the way in which Popkess writes about it suggests that he, and by extension Nottingham City Police, were certainly some of the forerunners of this way of thinking.

As part of this discussion on traffic flow and movement, Popkess investigated issues caused by the parking of vehicles at the side of the road "by motorists who are either thoughtless or selfish", and discussed how a driver "will complain at having to park his vehicle and walk several hundred yards" and as such inconvenience or hinder others. He highlighted how cars parking on both sides of a road can reduce traffic flow to one direction, and weighed up the benefits and drawbacks of parallel versus angle parking. He discussed the issue of disruptive on-street parking, and told how one or two vehicles parking inconsiderately can cause great inconvenience to hundreds of others.

Popkess' research on these traffic issues in the City was very well-informed, and on one occasion in the mid 1950s he was even known to have surveyed the city's traffic issues from the air, using the relatively new helicopter to help aid his understanding of its problems (see pages 117-118).

In a completely non-policing innovation, to combat the issue of inconsiderate parking he proposed introducing off-street car parks, explaining how they should be in places convenient for business people and shoppers and be fee free – or at the very least be moderately priced and offer season tickets to regular users. This proposal came at a time where such car parks were not common, with only a few in existence, and almost all parking was on-street. It could therefore be suggested that Popkess also helped to develop the concept of car parks; again, something that today almost seems that it has always existed and not been 'invented'.

It also wasn't until the Road Traffic and Roads Improvement Act 1960 that single and double yellow lines were introduced in an effort to combat such parking issues. Whilst he made no mention of such a solution in his book, it was well known that Ernest Marples, then Minister of Transport, and Capt Popkess were in regular correspondence – particularly over on-street parking issues – so it is entirely plausible that he and Popkess discussed and analysed the pros and cons of such an initiative.

The principle reason for Mr Marples and Capt Popkess corresponding with one another was over another innovation introduced in the Road Traffic Act 1960, as a result of one of Popkess' most high-profile ideas: Traffic Wardens.

Prior to the 1960 Act, enforcement of parking offences was the responsibility of local police forces. As Popkess detailed in an article he wrote for the *Police Journal* in April 1959 titled "Traffic Wardens: Food for Thought", this meant officers were abstracted from their normal beat duties to wait with offending vehicles for the drivers to return.

Fixed penalty notices did not exist at this time, which meant the only way to deal with inconsiderate parking was by reporting the offending driver for summons. This could mean waiting for two or more hours for the driver to return and be identified, during which time the constable could not undertake any other duties about his beat area.

Popkess did acknowledge that Traffic Wardens were not his idea, with a similar position already existing in South Africa and Australia. He had, however, researched into them and how they were utilised in their native countries, then transforming and adapting these functions into a uniquely British role.

Popkess' proposal was to introduce "a body of men, eager for police work, but barred by height or age to deal with trifling motoring offences like illegal parking and obstruction..."[37]

This was initially proposed on a local scale in Nottingham in 1958, and was presumed to be agreed by the time Popkess wrote his article. There was, however, a significant delay in introducing the scheme in Nottingham, when following a disagreement with Popkess the City Council declared that any funding for Traffic Wardens would have to come from the already existing police budget – in essence reducing the number of constables.

Ultimately, both London and Birmingham were to both get

37 *Sydney Morning Herald*, May 3rd 1959 pp. 78

Traffic Wardens before Nottingham's first cohort finally hit the streets on 20th January 1964, instantly being hailed a success, un-snarling Nottingham's previously heavily-congested city streets.[38] This was sadly some four years after Popkess' retirement in which he moved to Torquay, and so he would not have seen their effect.

Where Traffic Wardens (or Civil Enforcement Officers) are now commonplace in today's urban centres, in 1959 no such position existed – in Britain at any rate. Popkess accurately surmised and predicted initial reactions to such a position in his very opening line of "Traffic Wardens" when he wrote "one realises that such a scheme as this is somewhat of a revolutionary one..." This certainly summed up initial reactions to the proposal, which were met with disdain by the increasingly car-loving public. Upon the announcement of their introduction, the new parking enforcers were given various derogatory nicknames by the press based on their uniforms adorned with yellow bands such as 'Yellow Perils', 'Wasps' and 'Busy Bees'.

However, it appears that following the introduction of the wardens in Nottingham, traffic flow improved considerably. Former PC David 'Dan' Hyndman, in his history of the Nottingham City Police between 1960-68 uses hyperbole to describe the change, when he says that "the result was electric. Traffic was running smoothly and there was no kerb side congestion. Buses ran to time for the first time in many years."

The introduction of traffic wardens and the resultant improvement in the reliability of traffic flow that they created at the time is even more keenly felt in today's ever-more congested urban centres. Their initial proposition and eventual introduction typifies Capt Popkess' contribution to policing in the United

---

38 Hyndman, David: *Nottingham City Police: A Pictorial History 1960–1968* p.48

Kingdom. His desire was to improve every aspect of the Police Force and society as a whole upon which the Police could have any impact. Many of the ideas outlined above may not necessarily have been his own, but Popkess reviewed the latest policing and other innovations from across the world and adapted them to fit the British policing and societal model. This philosophy was not limited to road traffic matters, but was applied by Popkess to all aspects of policing.

Another foreign initiative that Popkess became aware of and expounded in Britain was that of radar speed detection – what we would today refer to as 'speed guns' or the more politically correct 'safety cameras'. In his *Police Journal* article from 1956 titled 'The Drunken Driver', the Captain devotes the latter half of the article not to drink driving but to "radar speed checks". He began, as per usual, by highlighting the problem that he wished to address. In this instance it was that in spite of ever-growing congestion on the roads, car manufacturers are making ever more powerful cars, capable of ever faster speeds.

In offering a solution, Popkess once again referred to America and inventions being tested there – specifically the use of 'Radar Speed Meters', whose use he wrote, had increased across the United States in the preceding three years. In another of his surprisingly accurate predictions of Twenty-first century life he wrote:

> "Speed limits… are often enforced more strictly [in America] than they are here. Sheer self-preservation has necessitated stronger controls and they are enforced with vigour and efficiency which we shall, no doubt, be forced to emulate in due course."

Of course today's motorists are almost united in their

displeasure at how vigorously and efficiently speed limits are enforced, but most would grudgingly accept that it is a necessary evil, proven to save lives and reduce road casualties – the very aim that Popkess was seeking to achieve.

Again, as with all his other proposed innovations, Popkess had a clear understanding of the science behind the proposal. He outlined in "Radar Speed Checks" about the British inventor of radar Sir Robert Watson Watt, and how it operated using the Doppler effect. He even detailed how the device is physically built, using what components and how it is mounted to the rear of a police car. He also cited statistical studies (what few there were at the time, given the relatively short period of time the technology had existed), showing that in sites with speed enforcement checks, serious and fatal collisions were reduced by more than half, and in some cases fatalities were dropping from 4-6 deaths a year to zero.

Popkess chose to quote passages in his article that highlighted the need for signage to warn of speed check sites, and also the need to only prosecute those significantly breaking the speed limit. It would seem clear that he understood the need to not enforce a zero-tolerance approach to the most minor of infractions, and the power of message re-enforcement through signage rather than simple roadside traps for the unsuspecting largely law-abiding motorist. This attitude is still the pervading one today when it comes to speed enforcement, with the legal requirement being to display signs at any fixed or regular mobile camera site. It appeared that Popkess knew that injury collisions were caused by those blatantly flouting the laws, rather than those who were possibly momentarily careless or inattentive.

As with so many of his other innovations, Popkess would

not live to see this one come to fruition. Police-operated speed detection equipment was not really seen in Britain until as late as the latter part of the 1980s, and the introduction of fixed cameras was not to be seen until 1992 – 36 years after Popkess extolled their virtues and sought their introduction.

Once again, this is yet another demonstration of just how far ahead of his time The Captain was, but how, because of that, he receives no credit for the seismic change in policing that speed cameras brought about. His contribution and input had been forgotten.

As can be seen, his contributions to road safety and traffic flow are considerable, and it is entirely possible that without some of these introductions today's cities would be permanently gridlocked and fatalities on the roads would be considerably higher. Of course, it is likely that someone else would have come up with similar or identical solutions to solve the problems, but they didn't; it was Popkess. He did not just research and propose solutions for one or two identified issues but a whole host of them, from a wide range of causes and backgrounds. It is in this area that his contribution to society as a whole perhaps goes most unrecognised. He was inducted into the Order of St John for his efforts in reducing road casualties, but it would appear a great injustice that he was not knighted for this combination of efforts into the area of Road Safety and Traffic flow improvements. Perhaps because he approached it from a policing perspective and his career ended in unfortunate circumstances, his name having been somewhat blackened, that he missed out on this accolade. It may also have been just how far ahead of his time he was with many of his initiatives that he simply lost the credit for them.

5

INNOVATIONS

It was not just in the field of road traffic that Capt Popkess innovated and brought about policing reform. Although that subject was clearly his passion both in terms of police use of motor vehicles and improvements around road safety and traffic flow, Popkess also revolutionised a plethora of other areas of policing.

In this chapter, many of those initiatives and ingenuities will be examined, providing further evidence towards the argument of Capt Popkess being the most influential figure on policing in the twentieth century.

These innovations not only highlight the genius of Popkess, but also served to really put Nottingham City Police on the proverbial map.

Former City Police officer Bob Rosamund puts it succinctly, stating that "it was *known* that Nottingham City Police was the best in the country, and possibly the world. There was a four-month waiting list to apply. Anyone who wanted to be a policeman in a decent force wanted to come to Nottingham."

Whilst there will always be a sense of pride in an officer's own force, Bob was not a native Nottinghamian, having moved to

Nottingham from London with the sole intention of joining the City's police force. He had to move up to the city and then get a temporary job for four months while he waited to start. It was the inspiration and innovations of Popkess and his officers that caused this national and international fame, and according to Rosamund was the primary reason that he both wanted to join the police, and Nottingham in particular.

One of the Captain's early innovations was the development of forensic science and purpose-built police laboratories. The period of Popkess' leadership of Nottingham City Police coincided with a hugely significant era of forensic advancement worldwide, and he was keen to incorporate all these new technologies into the pursuit of criminality. As with his inspiration for developments in Roads Policing, Popkess researched and borrowed ideas from other countries to aid his advances in forensic science.

As early into his tenure as 1933, Popkess went on visits to "all the important police laboratories in Europe" in order to study their methods, procedures and practices.[39]

His establishment of the Nottingham City Police Forensic Laboratory was a direct result of this fact-finding mission. The laboratory was the only one of its kind in the country; police forces previously utilising very little in the way of forensic technology, and that which they did would be paid for from external providers. Popkess argued against such an approach when he wrote about his fact-finding mission in an article entitled 'Pursuit by Science' published in the *Police Journal* in 1935. In this he argued that using external laboratories meant "the police in this country are not properly equipped scientifically".

39 *Nottingham Evening Post*, 22nd November 1934, p.10

After having reached that conclusion, Popkess caused Nottingham City Police to deviate from that practice. In early 1934 he opened the country's first Police Forensic Laboratory within the new Central Police Station on North Church Street. The Metropolitan Police were to follow only shortly after, with just the one laboratory for the entire force, and not opening theirs formally until 1935.[40]

This meant that forensic work in Nottingham could now be done quickly and comparatively cheaply 'in-house'. Furthermore, much of the forensic work was undertaken for free by students forming a part of their study. Some students from one of Nottingham's two higher education establishments even travelled from as far afield as Palestine in order to learn and develop their skills in the lab, where they worked with a full-time staff consisting of a biologist, chemist, physicist and microscopist.[41]

After being open less than a year, the benefit of the forensic laboratory in Nottingham was evident to the Home Office, who appointed it as their first national police laboratory – opening it up for other forces to send their samples and requests there for analysis.

Although the use of DNA in policing may not have begun until 1986, that is not the be-all and end-all of forensic science in the field of criminology. As has already been seen in *Roads Policing*, the laboratory was testing blood samples from suspected drink-drivers well in advance of any finite limits being set in law. The laboratory would also examine stains on clothing to establish their nature; bank notes and coins to establish if they were

---

40 Emsley, Clive: *A Police Officer and a Gentleman* (London: Blue Lamp Books 2018).
41 Popkess, Athelstan: "Pursuit by Science" in *The Police Journal: Theory, Practice and Principles* Volume 8, 2 (1st April 1935) p. 200.

forgeries; fingerprints; fibre and hair samples; blood group analysis; handwriting analysis and recording of tool marks amongst other things.

Not only was the establishment of the laboratory itself innovative, but the work undertaken by the staff there in the field of criminal forensics also drove innovation in the science itself. In 'Pursuit by Science', Popkess detailed how the laboratory staff, even as early as just over a year since opening, were experimenting with the use of spectrography (varying wave lengths of light in different substances) for policing purposes. Popkess cited examples of how the wave lengths of light in the blood of someone who has died from gas poisoning vary hugely to those of a normal person; how the trousers of a coal miner vary from those of a carpenter; and how different metals have different wave lengths. Using this method, the capture of a 'meter thief' is detailed by comparing microscopic flecks of paint on a tool found at the suspect's house to those on the attacked meter.

The expert enlarging of fingerprints for comparison was also furthered in the Nottingham City Police laboratory in its early years. Prior to this point, recovered fingerprints had to be photographed and then the film negatives enlarged during their development. Popkess stated that this method could take four hours, and be relatively expensive. The method devised by the police laboratory enlarged the image straight on to paper in less than a minute and at very little cost. The laboratory developed and then commissioned a new machine which was professionally made and subsequently named 'The Nottingham Fingerprint Reproducer'. This wasn't to be the only time that Popkess was influential in developing technology in-house for policing purposes which would be replicated nationally, and was probably not even the best example of it. That is to follow in the chapter 'The Mechanized Division'.

Popkess also noted the method used abroad of making plaster casts of injuries to reproduce them in court, and adapted this to fit the detection of burglaries in which tool marks were left. Casts would be made of the mark left by a tool using an extremely fine dental putty, and then using this 'negative' a 'positive' recreation of the mark would be made, allowing comparison against any tools found on arrested suspects. Similar was done with any footprint impressions.

Writing 'Pursuit by Science' just over a year following the inauguration of the Nottingham City Police laboratory, Popkess was already able to detail several heinous cases in which the offenders were brought to justice through the work of the forensic scientists:

- A male responsible for a violent indecent assault on a 7-year-old girl in Colwick Woods was convicted on evidence of seminal stains on his trousers, fragments of coarse woodland grass and ivy leaf on his trousers consistent with those at the scene of the crime, and human hairs identical to those of the victim on his coat, as well as evidence of gonorrhoea on his person which the victim also developed.

- A male struck on the head and severely wounded by a lump of coal subsequently found in the possession of another male involved in the disorder, and which was found to have blood of an identical group to the victim and a hair identical to that of the victim on it.

- An attempted rape of three small girls in a neighbouring force in which the suspect's clothes were found to bear the hair of a dog that the children were walking at the time of the offence, as well as grass identical to that growing at the scene of the crime. The children's clothes were also found to have fibres from the offender's scarf thereon.

- Conversely, the demonstrating that a different indecent assault allegation was in fact false after stains on a girl's underwear were found not to be semen, which led to the named suspect being released without charge.

- A murderer convicted with the assistance of the forensics team, after epithelial scales (a type of skin cell) were found in fingernail scrapings from the suspect which may have been from the victim's mouth when a handkerchief was shoved in it, as well as hair and fibres found at the scene of the crime and on the offender's coat.

- A burglar who committed a series of break-ins in Nottingham using a particular tool, and who initially evaded capture. Tool mark impressions were taken, and when a male was arrested in another part of the country in possession of a housebreaking tool and with a M.O. matching this series of burglaries, an officer was dispatched from Nottingham with the casts. When it matched exactly the prisoner promptly confessed to the Nottingham offences.

- A burglar who left his blood at the scene of one crime and a bloody glove at another was later arrested for loitering with intent. When it was pointed out to him that the blood group of both blood samples were the same as his, he promptly confessed to both offences.

The importance of having removed these offenders and demonstrating the innocence of another cannot be overstated. While it was entirely possible that items would have been sent off to an external laboratory in these cases, the specialist expertise of the police laboratory and the speed at which they were able to process the evidence has to have contributed to the far more expeditious course of justice in these cases. It is of particular note that in the case of the neighbouring forces, they chose to send in their evidence and place their faith in the Nottingham City Police laboratory rather than any other provider.

The key point that shines through 'Pursuit by Science' is the pride that Popkess had in the work of his laboratory, and the successes that have come as a result of its work; and it would certainly appear that he is entirely justified in that feeling. It is possible that the success of this earliest of his initiatives was what spurred him on to continue with his innovating.

***

Catching burglars by the use of forensic science after the event was certainly a significant step forward for policing, and enabled the detection of more of these traumatic offences. But Popkess wanted more. The key principle of Sir Robert Peel when founding the modern police service stipulated that:

"The basic mission for which police exist is to prevent crime and disorder as an alternative to the repression of crime and disorder".

In essence, then, catching a burglar after the fact was all well and good, but what if that burglar could be caught in the very act itself, or even before achieving it?

This was a question to which Popkess turned his attention after the conclusion of the Second World War. The result was the direct police burglar alarm.

Now commonplace in homes, businesses, cars and even garden sheds, it was in Nottingham in 1947 that the burglar alarm first

A still image of Popkess checking a burglary report taken from Pathé newsreel footage.

came into being. The Nottingham City Police system comprised of electrical contacts on closed doors, or a series of wires strung across the inside of windows in key premises, that if contact was lost or the wire knocked – by someone opening the door or climbing in through the window, for example – this would trigger a telegraphic signal to the police control room. This signal would cause a teleprinter therein to begin printing details of the location attacked and even specifically which window or door the signal had come from. This printout would then be handed to the radio controller, who would disseminate the information to all the nearby wireless radio-equipped mechanized vehicles. Officers could be on scene within minutes of the break-in occurring and thereby catch offenders in the act.

The simplicity of this design and co-ordinated police work is not only easy to describe and envision, but there exists a film demonstration of it, such was its perceived importance at the time.

A British Pathé newsreel – the '10 o'clock News' of its day – beautifully captured the whole sequence being demonstrated, complete with wonderful 1940s narration. The two minutes of footage is not only excellent for demonstrating the efficiency of the system, but also shows numerous different aspects of the City Police in the late 1940s, not to mention providing a little light-hearted humour when viewed from a twenty-first century perspective: "Bill Sykes doesn't know it, but the police teleprinter has him taped."

This wonderful snapshot of the Nottingham City Police force can be found online for free (at time of publishing) on the British Pathé website.[42]

It almost goes without saying that Popkess also wrote about the invention in an article entitled 'Police Co-Operation with a Burglar Alarm System' published in the January 1948 edition of the *Police Journal*.

***

Popkess did not just limit himself to grand projects such as his forensic laboratory, but also took significant time to research and attempt to better the investigation of myriad 'smaller' matters as well.

His pantheon of *Police Journal* articles, many of which have already been mentioned, also included writings on subjects as disparate as forged currency and stolen bicycles.

---

42 www.britishpathe.com/video/new-police-alarm-to-fight-theft-wave

Each of these articles represented a considerable amount of Popkess' time given over to their research and writing. As with his larger, more ambitious projects, they also possibly represented a seismic change in operational day-to-day policing, but just not on such a grand scale. Several of the articles linked into one another, or spun out of his other initiatives. An article entitled 'The Teleprinter and the Man on the Beat', published in the April 1955 edition, clearly stemmed from his work on burglar alarms combined with his work on the Mechanised Division, seeking how to incorporate the functions of a teleprinter to patrol officers. It could be argued that this foresight for wanting officers to have access to more comprehensive information whilst on patrol has developed today into the use of mobile devices issued to officers. This allows them access to police force systems remotely anywhere that they happen to be.

Clearly, technology such as this was inconceivable to Popkess in the time period he was in charge, but his desires seemingly laid the groundwork for it.

Another of his articles, 'Classification of Handwriting and Counterfeit Coins', published in July 1934 clearly coincides with the launch of the force's new Forensic Laboratory. His research into this article must have come out of part of his research into the forensics around that subject area. The fact that Popkess managed to find the time to write the article concurrently with launching the new forensics facility, as well as monitoring that and writing about its results, shows the strength of his character, and just how passionate he was about each and every subject that he came across. The fact that he chose to write about it then, and not wait until his work on the laboratory had calmed down, demonstrates that he was also passionate about catching criminals – he didn't want to risk any evading capture if publishing his work sooner could help catch them.

Perhaps inspired by his experiences after catching Blackwater whilst serving in the First World War, in 1952 he wrote an article about the effects of Morphia on its users. More commonly known as heroin today, the adverse effects of opiates on its habitual users were becoming more and more known, and Popkess wrote about these from a policing perspective.

***

As almost a postscript, it would be rude and remiss to discuss all these innovations of Capt Popkess in this chapter without giving credit to Deputy Chief Constable George Downs.

As could perhaps be inferred from the huge variety of innovations conceived of and introduced by Popkess, coupled with his penchant for writing, there was very little time left for the actual operational running of the force itself.

This day-to-day leadership was very much left to DCC Downs, who took the helm of the operational aspects, allowing Popkess to nurture, develop and finalise his initiatives, as well as to then write them up and disseminate them. It could easily be argued that, without Downs' surrogate leadership, Popkess would not have been able to innovate to anywhere near the same degree. But perhaps it was similarly testament to Popkess that he had such confidence in his recruitment policies, standing orders, and his leadership team, that he was content to let the force operate in his name and remove himself to an extent from the operational aspects. By any reckoning, Downs and Popkess made a formidable leadership pairing that truly enabled Nottingham City Police to flourish under their command, and Downs' willingness to go above and beyond simply being a 'deputy' enabled Popkess to become such a visionary and truly develop and modernise Policing. This was to continue with Downs' replacement Thomas Moore, who was eventually to succeed Popkess as chief following his retirement. Such was their close working relationship that Moore would later address his former boss with the very familiar almost pet name of 'Pop' when writing to him in his retirement.[43]

What could be identified as Popkess' largest and most important innovation has not yet been covered in this chapter, but so wholesale and groundbreaking were the results of this advancement that it fundamentally revolutionised policing. When these overarching combination of initiatives and practices are taken together it is arguable that they, more than any other definable aspect of twentieth century policing, mark the epoch-shift in British law enforcement from the traditional Victorian-era beat system to the modern Twenty-first Century police force.

Capt Popkess himself, only two years after launching this innovation, wrote that:

> "The effect of [it] upon the speeding-up of the whole police system of the city, and the saving of many thousands of hours of patrol time, will be too evident to require comment."[44]

It is for this reason that Popkess' creation, development and continual refinement of the Mechanized Division warrants a chapter of its own.

43 The National Archives: HO 272/83. Letter dated 17th March 1961 from 'Tom' to Popkess.
44 Popkess, Athelstan: "Nottingham City Police Wireless" in *The Police Journal: Theory, Practice and Principles* Volume 7, 2 (1st April 1934) p. 150.

6.

THE MECHANIZED DIVISION

Today's nostalgic image of a police constable may still be that of an officer in a black tunic with silver buttons wearing the familiar 'custodian' helmet. But in truth, it is far more likely to see a police officer, male or female, driving past in a car wearing a flat cap or, more likely, no headwear at all. We may get a fleeting glimpse of their stab vest over a black polo shirt or a fleece. They will also have a secure two-way radio clipped to their top, giving them instant communication with their central control room. Officers are able to summon help in an emergency with the press of a single button.

Life was very different for police officers between the wars. When the new Chief Constable took over in 1930 it would have been a rare sight to see a policeman in a car. The few police women in the force at the time certainly didn't drive cars at all. It wasn't to be until the late 1950s that Policewoman 18 Mary Needham became the first female officer in Nottingham permitted to drive for policing duties. This occasion was of such significance that a publicity photograph was arranged in front of the Central Police Station. After the photograph was taken Capt Popkess himself emerged from the building, unaware of the staged situation which had just taken place outside. He promptly climbed into the rear of

Publicity photograph showing Policewoman Mary Needham behind the wheel

the car, believing it was there for him and had PW Needham take him to the bank and back again, apparently none-the-wiser. The Chief's normal drivers from the Mechanized Division apparently failed to see the funny side of it.[45]

In 1930 the Nottingham City force had only a handful of vehicles, and those were only used for senior officers and in emergencies. The working day for a constable was spent pounding the beat. The speed of a police response was limited to how fast an officer could run, if one could even be located nearby by a victim. If an officer needed assistance they could only hope that their whistle

45 Phillips, Robert & Andrews, Tom: *100 Years of Women in Policing Nottingham* p. 27

would be heard and bring colleagues from neighbouring beat areas running to their aid.

To contact his commanders, an officer would have to find one of the police telephone boxes scattered around the city. He would be expected to check in regularly in this way so that instructions could be passed, and his sergeant could be reassured that nothing untoward had happened to him.

It didn't take long after Popkess' arrival in the force for the ex-military man to see how speeding up communications and mobility for officers on patrol could radically change the effectiveness of his team.

Forming a wholly new and revolutionary Mechanized Division was among the first of his actions in Nottingham, and Popkess worked tirelessly to implement it, conducting pioneering experiments in radio communications. The changes he brought about proved to be some of the most influential innovations in the history of policing in Britain.

It was as early as January 1933, only three years into his tenure, that Captain Popkess had his very first article published in the *Police Journal*: 'Pursuit by Wireless: The Value of Mobility'. The article goes into detail about Popkess' experiments with the introduction of wireless technology in Nottingham City Police, and the introduction of motor patrols within the force.

The fact that this was only three years after he took the helm of Nottingham City Police, really gives an indication of the strength of Popkess' passion for the field of roads policing and mechanisation. That he felt confident he was in a position to publish his results as an example nationally after so comparatively short a time shows that he must have introduced this idea almost immediately upon taking the helm.

Popkess began by identifying the requirement for the Mechanized Division, writing that:

"The days when the majority of our criminals were locals whose methods and haunts were well known to local police personnel are rapidly going... methods must be brought up to date to cope with rapidly changing conditions."[46]

The article then goes on to detail how Nottingham City Police had trialled the most efficient means of deploying and tasking the mobile patrols that the force had discovered.

Such was the success of Popkess' efforts, and so pioneering was his work at the time on a national level, that the Chief Constable ultimately wrote and published another of his books on the subject in order that the details of his experiments and the resultant best practice could be disseminated across the country to other police forces. Popkess wrote *Mechanised Police Patrol* in an apparent desire to significantly expand on and bring together his various *Police Journal* essays around the subject, which included:

- 'Pursuit by Wireless' from 1933
- 'Nottingham City Police Wireless' from 1934
- 'Police Co-Operation with a Burglar Alarm System' from 1948
- 'Judging Speed by Skid Marks' from 1949

First published in 1949, then updated and revised in 1954, in 163 A5 pages *Mechanised Police Patrol* details every aspect of how mechanised, wireless radio-equipped policing worked best,

46 'Pursuit by Wireless: The value of mobility' Popkess, Athelstan in *The Police Journal: Theory, Practice and Principles* Volume 6,1 (1st January 1933) p. 31

based on his extensive testing in Nottingham.[47] It would seem likely that the book was delayed by at least six years as a result of the Second World War, given that Popkess had been trialling the processes since 1930 and first written about it in 1933. The technological advances during the War no doubt also significantly increased the abilities of the wireless radios.

Mechanised Police Patrol covers every aspect of the efficient running of a Mechanized Division, from police vehicle roadworthiness, to how best to deploy resources; radio etiquette to pre-arranged tactics. Popkess outlined all these different facets, clearly satisfied that his own force had reached optimum performance following his various trials.

The book begins by looking at routine maintenance of police vehicles, and the responsibilities of the police drivers to conduct checks of their vehicles before each tour of duty. Such an idea will sound very familiar even to serving officers of today, who are still required to do basic checks of their patrol vehicles at the commencement of a tour of duty. Popkess was the first Chief Constable to demand this, and this is another of his initiatives that has survived through the ages, having proved its worth.

Popkess' initiatives may now be taken for granted as standard practice, but what is crucial to bear in mind is that they remain standard practice some half a century later, due to the rigorous trials conducted by The Captain and Nottingham City Police. This is perhaps best exampled in the tests the force undertook with wireless telegraphy and telephony, whilst pioneering the use of the wireless radio.

This work on the development of the use of radios within the police was one of Capt Popkess' first and perhaps most

---

47 Popkess, Athelstan: *Mechanised Police Patrol* Barnicotts Ltd: Somerset (1954).

Nottingham City Police uniform cruiser PC 91 Wigg with a radio pack.

groundbreaking innovations. There is a strong argument it is also his most important and lasting legacy, given the modern ubiquity and absolute necessity for the use of radios by the emergency services.

It is again an aspect of policing and everyday life in professions from bus driving to construction, now so commonplace it is hard to think of it as ever having been 'invented' at all. It may not necessarily have all started with Popkess, but it was he who seized on the emerging technology and developed it to an operational level of excellence.

His reasons for pioneering this new way of working were expressly conveyed by him from the outset in Pursuit by Wireless, when he outlined that

> "Mobility, mechanization and communication will be considered in relation to each other, for there can be no real mobility unless they are closely related, and each is as efficient

as we can make it".[48]

Popkess had clearly identified from the beginning that it is not possible to have the enhanced mobility and speed of using cars to transport officers around unless you can direct them to those incidents in a similarly quick manner.

He recognised that having his newly-mobile officers staying at base, deploying to incidents and then returning again, reduced their efficiency dramatically by increasing travelling time. It meant the ability to deploy them elsewhere immediately upon completion of the preceding incident was lost. It also drastically undermined one of Sir Robert Peel's founding principles for the police of a visible patrolling deterrent.

Marconi had invented the wireless radio systems of Telephony (speech) and Telegraphy (Morse Code) twenty years previously in 1909, and Popkess was certainly not the first to pair the relatively new technology with police work.

John Bunker describes initial testing with radio receivers fitted to mobile vans by the Metropolitan Police in his book *From Rattle to Radio*. He gives examples from 1924, when the Met tested a mobile vehicle capable of transmitting and receiving, and then in 1925 how they equipped the recently formed Flying Squad vans with a wireless telegraphy receiver.[49]

Popkess did not begin at the helm of Nottingham City Police until 1930, but almost immediately began trials and experiments with the use of both telegraphic and telephonic systems. His aim, in parallel to that of the Met, was to establish the best system and best practice for its integration into policing.

---

48 'Pursuit by Wireless' p. 31
49 Bunker, John: *From Rattle to Radio* Brewin Books: Surrey (1988) pp. 158-170

Popkess appears to have achieved this better than anything else contemporary to him being developed, or certainly made much more of his research and experiments. As with his other innovations he wrote extensively on the subject, thereby disseminating it further across the policing landscape of the time. It was this desire to disseminate his research for the betterment of policing nationally that led to his publishing of *Mechanised Police Patrol* as the culmination of his various *Police Journal* articles. Somewhat bizarrely, Bunker seems to almost completely overlook Popkess' research and contribution, in a very Metropolitan Police-centric manner, as with so much history of the British police. The only mention Nottingham gets is a passing reference to when the man tasked with introducing wireless communication to the Metropolitan Police visited various other forces and found that "at this time Nottingham was the most advanced of those provincial forces visited."

In his very first year at the helm of the City Police Popkess established the Mechanized Division – his South African ancestry no doubt accounting for the use of the non-vernacular 'z'! Within three years he was fitting all 39 vehicles of the Division with wireless, meaning all officers therefore had to be proficient in its use. In contrast with the Metropolitan force at the same time, only 38 constables there were trained in the use of wireless equipment, which was only fitted on 22 vehicles across that entire force and predominantly limited to the Flying Squad.[50]

The Captain was well aware of the pioneering role that Nottingham City Police was playing, writing in 'Pursuit by Wireless' that he had to carefully consider whether to embark or telegraphy or telephony as

---

50 Bunker, John: *From Rattle to Radio* Brewin Books: Surrey (1988) pp. 158-170

"We found ourselves the first in the field in what we were attempting to obtain – two-way communication between a mobile unit and its Headquarters."

This is what perhaps inspired Popkess to write up his results; to help others overcome this issue he had encountered. It is certainly quite bizarre to think that in the ten-year head-start the Metropolitan Police had over Nottingham, it seems that no-one there had considered or at least given serious thought to the possibility of two-way communication with deployed units. Presumably they had found some success with the experiments in one-way communication with the Flying Squad for the experimenting to continue, but with no suggestion of expanding this to other teams or for more wider police work.

Interestingly, and perhaps counter-intuitively to today's view, Popkess concluded that telegraphy was the preferred method of communication by wireless, rather than the far easier method of telephony now in use universally. He explains in 'Pursuit By Wireless' that whilst the spoken word of telephony meant that "it was not necessary for personnel to learn Morse, and it had speed and simplicity of transmission", it had "certain disadvantages for police purposes". These he gives as the absence of secrecy, interference from ordinary civilian broadcast systems, severe distortion and the technical difficulties of fitting the cars with a significantly larger and more expensive system able to both transmit and receive. The telegraphic wireless unit replaced the entire passenger seat as it was, and could just about be fitted in motorbike side-cars; whereas there was a reason that the telephonic systems being trialled in the Metropolitan Police had to be installed in a van. Telegraphy tape machine units could also be installed in "static units such as [police divisional] sub-stations and [police] phone boxes". Surprisingly, Popkess also concluded that whilst it would be expected that telegraphy might be slower than telephony, "actual experience has since shown this not to be so".[51] Watching Morse operators, and seeing the speeds with which Morse messages could be relayed in the Second World War, it is possible to see why this might actually have been the case.

Popkess used the freedom and speed enabled by the use of radio to great effect, and in a wholly different way to the early philosophy of his London colleagues. In 'Pursuit by Wireless: The Value of Mobility' he explains how the Mechanized Division patrolled nine designated areas superimposed over the already existing 60 foot beat areas, thereby increasing the patrol cover across the City. Through this method he enabled the use of the radios to the force as a whole, rather than limiting it to one elite specialist squad in the way that the Met had. Not only could the messages be relayed directly to the Mechanized units, they could then pass these on to local patrolling 'foot beat' officers within their respective overlapping operational patrol areas.

Former officer Bob Rosamund remembers fondly that instead of being disliked or seen as elitist, the Mechanized Division was well-liked by officers on 'foot beat' divisions. He remembers particularly how grateful beat officers were for the speed which the Mechanized officers could back them up at incidents, especially in the days before personal radios. He gives an example of when an officer was in trouble and a member of the public who saw him struggling with someone called the main police number, and Mechanized units were dispatched and on scene within minutes. The only enmity occurred between those with police cars and those without, when the Mechanized officers would invariably hand jobs over to foot beat officers. Nothing apparently changes,

---

51 'Pursuit by Wireless' p. 38

with Traffic and Armed Response departments often (allegedly) continuing similar practices today!

This use of mobile patrols in addition to the foot patrol areas meant that officers on the Mechanized Division could be dispatched to a call by means of wireless radio, and if necessary collect beat officers in their vehicles en-route to incidents that needed greater numbers. The Mechanized officers could also relay more urgent messages to beat officers in advance of that officer's scheduled 'check-in' time at a Police Box or with a sergeant.

The overlaying of the Mechanized Patrol areas on top of the beat areas is still familiar today. Certainly within today's Nottinghamshire Police, local neighbourhood beat areas which are covered by officers on foot patrol are overlaid with larger emergency response areas covered by officers in low-powered police vehicles covering several beats. These in turn are overlaid with force-wide and regional specialist teams (firearms, traffic etc), who patrol areas using faster, high-powered vehicles. Other forces have local response areas, covered by fast response 'area cars' as well, but this scaled cover principle is replicated nationally across today's police forces. The initial idea of overlaying smaller local policing beat areas with larger ones comprising more mobile officers, however, began in Nottingham City in 1930 at the direction of Chief Constable Popkess, and is yet another example of his visionary forward-thinking becoming the 'industry standard', even nearly a century later.

This need for the overlaying of beat areas and Mechanized Division patrol areas meant that a method had to be devised in order to convey only relevant messages to the patrolling Mechanized Division units, rather than inundate all the radio-equipped officers with messages not relevant to them and their patrol area. Again Popkess provided a solution for the problem that his experimenting had created. In 'Pursuit by Wireless' Popkess outlines how he divided the city's Motor Patrol Areas into three separate radio areas each operating on their own unique frequency, controlled from one of three wireless stations. This is yet again a police radio usage principle still followed today, termed a radio talkgroup area, showing how Popkess' solution to his identified problem was one that has not needed any further amendments some 85 years later.

***

Popkess did not stop at simply introducing the wireless communications and Mechanized Division with its overlapping structure. He also developed tactics to best utilise this new-found mobility and speed in various policing scenarios. He does this by again citing successful examples from the Nottingham City force, as he did with the success of his forensics laboratory:

- One of the most recognisable of these tactics developed is the description of what in today's policing world would be described as a 'snatch plan', or a 'code blue' in modern Nottinghamshire Police parlance. Following reports of a burglary or robbery in progress, the control room direct all available units to key locations in an effort to contain the area and prevent the offender getting away. This is not a new idea, and in fact originated with Popkess. In Pursuit by Wireless he writes about a situation where a woman had her bag snatched by a thief in the street in a Nottingham residential housing estate. She requested a nearby resident call the police, and Mechanized Division cars were dispatched immediately. Each car was allocated to one of the five exits of the estate, and within four minutes of the instructions being transmitted every location was blocked. Sadly, in this instance no suspect was apprehended, but this is a perfect example of Popkess' new tactics in action, and the speed at which they could be implemented, possibly even faster than today.

- In a similar incident with a variation on these tactics, a woman had called in to the police to say she had seen an intruder in her hallway and provided a good description of him. Vehicles from the Mechanized Division were mobilised and collected numerous other officers en route to the scene, enabling the surrounding streets to be swamped with officers. This resulted in the arrest and subsequent conviction of the male, who also confessed to several other burglaries.

- He also highlights a case when a stolen car from Derby was believed to be heading to Nottingham and a radio message was passed to the motor patrols, resulting in the vehicle being sighted and stopped and the occupants arrested within twelve minutes of the message being received from Derby Police. This type of message would now be universally recognised as an 'observations message' or 'BOLO' (Be On the Look Out) and is commonplace in modern policing.

- A further example demonstrates another one of the innovations Popkess introduced as part of the Mechanized Division: "Special Mission Patrols". These were described as "special duties carried out by vehicles camouflaged as tradesmen's vans, etc", and are to be tasked to "patrol residential districts where there are epidemics of daylight breaks-in" and similar taskings. The drivers of these Special Mission Patrols would also be in plain clothes. Popkess calls these vehicles "'Q' Cruisers' – a term still used in the Metropolitan Police today. The use of undercover officers was certainly not new, and dates back almost to the creation of the police service, but the use of vehicles to assist with pro-active policing – especially equipped with wireless radios – most certainly was. One example that Popkess gives in *Pursuit by Wireless* is of a Q Cruiser sighting a stolen vehicle after observations were passed for it and then engaging in a pursuit with it relaying commentary of the pursuit, and eventually resulting in the offenders being caught.

Such was his eagerness to prove the abilities of his new tactics, especially in relation to the use of his Observations Messages and the rapid deployment of his mobile resources, that early in their creation, Popkess was keen to put them to the test. In September of 1932, still early into the Mechanized Division's establishment, the wireless-equipped patrols were dispatched to reports of a suspected stolen car seen on the streets of the City. As the mobile patrols located and pulled up alongside the vehicle, they were amazed to see the laughing face of none other than their Chief Constable at the wheel of the 'stolen' vehicle! Popkess had had the wireless operators put out the erroneous message so that he could experience first-hand the abilities of his new department.[52]

Popkess' experiments had proved a huge success, but one issue he discovered was that his Mechanized Division vehicles were often hampered getting around by other traffic. Prior to this introduction, police vehicles may have been fitted with a bell or simply had no warning noise at all, but the tests found that even the bell was not great at alerting other road users. To overcome this problem, Popkess instructed that tests be conducted on fitting *sirens* to the vehicles. These tests discovered that "the rising and falling crescendo of these alarms had the effect of clearing a crowded street very expeditiously... These sirens will only be used in emergencies..."[53] The 'rising and falling' siren noise and their use only in emergency situations are also still

52 *Sheffield Daily Telegraph*, 27th September 1932, p.3.
53 'Pursuit by Wireless' p. 35.

current practice today, and show no signs of disappearing. Yet another aspect of policing taken for granted today, but which was invented by Popkess.

Popkess' experiments and success with wireless communications and the Mechanized Division were so influential to his contemporaries that he was prompted to write a second *Police Journal* article just over a year later. The opening lines of 'Nottingham City Police Wireless' give an indication of what prompted him to write it so soon after his previous work:

> "Since the publication of my article 'Pursuit by Wireless' ... so many inquiries have been received as to the kind of work done by our wireless patrols..."[54]

The article goes on to list several examples of radio telegraphy messages transcribed by the HQ radio operator, to give examples of typical daily activities performed by the Mechanized units. These messages in full are reproduced in Appendix 2.

Some of these messages are almost mundane by today's standards, with many being requests for units to attend a location for an 'area search' for suspicious persons reported with replies of 'no trace' after an hour or so of looking. These are bread and butter incidents for police officers today asked to search for a group of youths causing anti-social behaviour or similar, but as has been the case with so many of his innovations, at the time of Popkess' writing it was groundbreaking.

Only a year prior to the introduction of the Mechanized Division, if a victim encountered a burglar in their house they would have had to shout out of their windows for the police and

---

54 'Nottingham City Police Wireless' Popkess, Athelstan in *The Police Journal: Theory, Practice and Principles* Volume 7,2 (1st April 1934) p. 147

hope the local beat officer was nearby. Alternatively, they could have telephoned the local police station and officers could have made their way from there. This would have taken time however to assemble the men from the station, and then additional time spent travelling to the scene. The officers would not have been able to receive any further updates whilst en route either.

With the introduction of the Mechanized Division and wireless radio, officers could be dispatched to the relevant address at the outset of the call, with updates such as descriptions etc, passed whilst officers were driving – reducing crucial delays in reaching the scene. Once again, it is the apparent mundanity of these exemplar messages to today's reader that speaks for just how integral and fundamental Popkess' pioneering innovation was to become.

The final transmission quoted in 'Nottingham City Police Wireless' gives another way in which Popkess' introduction of wireless, coupled with mobility, moved the police service forwards. The final exampled messages read:

"15.10.33. From No. 3 Patrol to H.Qs.
23.33. Am standing by for communication purposes at big fire Basford"

Again, this may not seem a significant communication, but it demonstrates a leap forward in how the police command structure could deal with large incidents.

Previously, a senior officer would have probably have needed to attend any significant incident in order to take command and oversee operations. This officer may have had to remain there a significant period of time, preventing them undertaking other duties.

With the introduction of wireless communications, the requirement for senior officers to be on scene on the ground vanished overnight. Now, those senior officers could remain anywhere wireless equipment was installed and be called upon to make decisions whenever the need arose. Outside of these times they could undertake their other core duties, significantly increasing their efficiency.

This ability has ultimately evolved into the 'gold, silver and bronze' command structure seen in emergency services today, where senior officers have no need to attend the scene of major incidents and are able to make decisions remotely based on information from officers at the scene passed by radio. It has ultimately also enabled a streamlining of higher ranks, with one senior officer being able to cover many more areas and be able to remotely manage multiple incidents at one time.

At the time of Popkess taking up his post, each division and even subdivision would have had a superintendent or chief superintendent holding the required authority to make key decisions at major incidents, all of whom would have had to be available for call-out at any time. Wireless communication changed all this, with only one senior officer being needed to make decisions at any and all incidents across the force.

***

Perhaps the most surprising aspect of all with regards to the development of the Mechanized Division, and why just so much credit is due Popkess rather than a wireless company that developed the system at his request, is that the whole undertaking was conducted 'in-house'.

In 'Pursuit by Wireless' Popkess detailed the setting up of the system along with the thought processes of telegraphy

v. telephony etc. He then explains how he initially contacted a "well-known firm of wireless manufacturers", outlining his plans, and how he was prepared to provide facilities in which their experiments could be conducted. Popkess then appears to have had an epiphany that "business houses are not exactly philanthropic institutions, and that it would be better to do the work ourselves if we could find somebody locally to advise us."

That person came in the form of a Mr H. B. Old, described by Popkess as 'an amateur experimenter'! In Mr Old, Popkess seems to have found someone as passionate about this idea as he was, explaining that Mr Old undertook the experiments and constructed the sets "free gratis", and that as a result "such success as we have had is due entirely to him".[55]

Popkess was not only revolutionising policing, he was doing it for free.

So successful were Capt Popkess and Mr Old's experiments and constructions that two years later, when "one of the foremost wireless manufacturers in this country, as the result of their attractive booklet on 'Police Wireless', was invited by the writer to have their wireless telephony outfit tried out in Nottingham under service conditions", the apparent market leaders failed at every task set of them. Two-way communications were not even able to be demonstrated, and broadcasts from HQ to the mechanized units were so laden with interference that the messages came through garbled and unintelligible. There was also an unfortunate by-product of significant interference with civilian BBC radio between 250-500 metres from the police transmitter.[56]

It appears that Nottingham City Police had in fact become the foremost manufacturers of police wireless communications in

55 'Pursuit by Wireless' pp. 38-39
56 'Nottingham City Police Wireless' pp.151-2

the country. No doubt the invited guests with their 'attractive booklet' left rather hurriedly with their tails between their legs.

This 'back-room boffin' attitude, supporting a charismatic leader to realise their goals, was to become typical of Britain's subsequent War effort. This pairing of Popkess and Old could be compared to that of Churchill and Barnes-Wallace who followed. It also goes a long way to explaining how Popkess was able to achieve so much. He was not reliant on large grants or convincing government budget holders to release funds to him in order to pay large external suppliers. His ideas were simple enough to be undertaken with existing force funding and completed in-house without resorting to established profit-making companies – who certainly in this instance provided a substandard service compared to a bespoke solution built from the ground up to suit the police's needs.

***

With the formation of the Mechanized Division and the increased use of police motor vehicles came the need for officers to uphold and exceed the standards expected of other road users. To this end, Popkess took great interest in the best system of car control allowing his Mechanized officers to drive progressively and safely.

Some training already existed for police drivers in advanced car control, under a system devised in the mid-1930s at the Metropolitan Police Driving School at Hendon by the Sixth Earl of Cottenham – racing driver Mark Pepys. This was, however, almost exclusively confined to Police Officers, and most specifically those in the Metropolitan force. Popkess researched and expounded the virtues of this system to his own officers, giving the training to all officers in the Mechanized Division.

In *Mechanised Police Patrol*, Popkess also brought Pepys' 'System of Car Control' to a wider audience, enabling anyone who read the book to learn and adopt the safe driving methods used by officers.

It is clear that Popkess was well aware of advanced systems of car control, even early into his time at the helm of Nottingham City Police. In 'Pursuit by Wireless' he highlighted a success of the Mechanized Division as a result of a police pursuit in which he describes that "on account of its unfavourable position, the police car overturned at a sharp turn". This shows that he was aware of how road positioning affected the stability of vehicles even as early as 1933, in parallel to Pepys' teaching of it at Hendon.

Nowadays, police officers and other advanced drivers would recognise this 'System' as being outlined in the book *Roadcraft*. However, the first recognisable edition of this was only published in 1954, whereas Popkess' book *Mechanised Police Patrol* was published in 1949.[57] It could therefore be argued that Popkess was innovative in bringing these advanced driving standards to a wide audience, including the general public, allowing anyone to become a safer driver. It must be the case that this desire to increase driving standards was borne out of The Captain's passion for road safety. By extension, the officers under his command must have been expected to be the epitome of these principles in the eyes others. Popkess was certainly the first Chief Constable to extend these highest standards of driving to *all* his officers who might drive vehicles for work purposes and

---

57 Initially released as Attention All Drivers! by Jock Taylor a former Hendon police driving instructor and rereleased a year later as Roadcraft www.police-foundation. org.uk/projects/roadcraft as accessed 21/11/2014

not simply a small elite.

Popkess did not rest on his laurels throughout his tenure, constantly striving to improve and update the technology and abilities of the Mechanized Division. In later years Popkess would introduce motorbike patrols which would latterly incorporate radios, as the technology improved and reduced in size. This technological improvement continued to the point that officers were issued personal issue radios towards the end of Popkess' tenure.

All the innovations in both the Mechanized Division and across the Nottingham City Police Force, conceived and borne to fruition under the supervision of Capt Popkess, changed the face of policing in the twentieth century and beyond. Numerous of these ideas are still standard practice nationwide today, such as:

- Escalating patrol areas from beat officer, through local response cop and divisional teams to regional resources;
- Daily vehicle checks;
- Local geographic and larger area radio 'talkgroups';
- 'Snatch plans';
- Police-linked burglar alarms;
- The securing, preserving and analysis of forensic evidence from road traffic collisions;
- Police advanced driving standards;
- Radio etiquette;
- Command and control radio dispatch to incidents
- Rising and falling (wailer) police sirens

All of the above would be instantly recognisable as still standard practice in the police force of today; but in the era of Popkess, they were all new. Whilst Popkess may not have specifically directly

Top: Motorbike radio test
Bottom: Officers testing personal issue radios

invented some of the items on the list (such as forensic science), he brought them to the fore and realised their policing potential, harmonising all these different aspects into a highly efficient and co-ordinated police force; one that was respected both nationally and internationally.

Former Chief Superintendent Silverwood reminisces that Popkess may not necessarily have been the origin of some of the advances, but that once an idea was mooted he would seize upon it and develop it to its introduction. His development of these innovations in mobility and communications, alongside the initiatives outlined in the previous chapters on Roads Policing and Innovations, really stand to mark Popkess out as the leading policing figure of the twentieth century.

Bizarrely for an area about which he was clearly so passionate, and which he pioneered on a national level, the Mechanized Division was not the pride of Popkess' City Police. Bob Rosamund remembers that the City Division covering Nottingham City Centre was in fact The Captain's favourite. Postings there were reserved for only the tallest and most athletic of officers, and invariably used by Popkess to showcase his force in sporting events, as well as HMIC inspections and publicity materials. It is perhaps because of his continual desire to always be prepared for every eventuality that he focussed his most 'elite' officers in the City Centre; where protests, riots, photo calls or any other eventuality had the highest likelihood of occurring. It is this Preparedness that the next chapter examines.

7.

PREPAREDNESS

Ask any Nottinghamian over a certain age what their endearing memory of the city's Old Market Square was, exclusive of its physical features, and their answer will invariably be PC Dennis Wilson – 'Tug' as he was most commonly known.

At 6' 8½" tall and sporting a 'walrus' moustache, the barrel-chested 'Tug' Wilson cut an imposing figure, standing on his almost constant vigil over his Old Market Square beat area, shared with his erstwhile companion, PC Geoffrey Baker, only very marginally shorter at 6' 8". Both PCs had been Grenadier Guardsmen, and that position, coupled with their commanding statures, had earned them positions as two of the eight pallbearers at the funeral of King George VI in 1952. They were subsequently awarded the Royal Victorian Medal, granted them personally by the Queen in thanks for their bearing her father's body into Westminster Abbey. Both soldiers were approached directly by Popkess, who had witnessed the giants carrying the deceased monarch's coffin, offering them employment with Nottingham City Police.

This approach towards these men, based solely on their stature and bearing, was absolutely typical of Popkess. Former officer Bob Rosamund, himself 6' 3" tall, recollects that only the very

Bob Rosamund

tallest officers above 6' 2" were permitted to serve on the City Division. This favouritism really instilled a sense of pride in those officers, privileged enough by fortune of birth to serve in the City. Their pride was reinforced by Popkess, who did not hide his preference for this division.

His background during the First World War in the Legion of Frontiersmen probably led him down this path, where he witnessed truly tough men acting heroically, with their sheer physical presence potentially cowing and intimidating their enemies. This was most likely The Captain's desire with his officers in the City and especially in the central Old Market Square. Having such tall and imposing officers towering over the heavily trafficked area would naturally draw the public's attention to this visible symbol of law and order. They provided a constant, subtle reminder that the police were watching over everyone, and created an illusion almost of omnipresence.

This was a relatively simple but effective policy on the part of Popkess to demonstrate policing control over the streets, and get 'value for money' from his resources: by placing the most visible ones in the busiest area, where they will be seen the most. This is a typical example of his entire philosophy whilst being at the helm of Nottingham City Police.

Simply put, Popkess did not want to be caught unawares. By having the most imposing officers in the country put in the most visible location of the City Centre, Popkess no doubt sought to quell any potential troubles before they even begun, through the 'intimidatory' presence of his policing giants, especially given that historically Nottingham had always been a hotbed of unrest for various reasons and causes. This hatred of being taken by surprise and having to react to events rather than seize the initiative and pro-actively prevent them also no doubt stemmed from Popkess' experiences during the First World War, where on the occasions that Popkess and his men were taken by surprise there were severe negative consequences. Conversely, he had also seen the success of being pro-active and taking the initiative in situations, such as executing the IRA man on his way to commit a bombing, thereby preventing large loss of life.

This desire to 'Be Prepared' ran like a seam through all of Popkess' policy and decision-making throughout his tenure at the helm in Nottingham. As a cultural aside, 'Be Prepared' is the motto of the Scout Organisation, which was founded in Britain in 1907 when Popkess was 14. Scouting's founder Lord Baden-Powell famously conceived of Scouting in South Africa during the Boer War during the Siege of Mafeking in 1899-1900, when he utilised the very savvy, hardy and world-wise local boys to act as messengers for his army unit, and wanted to bring such outdoor skills and self-reliance to British boys. These events were taking place at the same time that Popkess was a boy, and his rugged childhood made him just such a youth, who but for a couple of years and a few hundred miles could have been one of those hardy boys at Mafeking. It was also this location and experience that lent Baden-Powell towards Rudyard Kipling's novels as a theme for his younger Cub Scouts movement. No doubt Popkess would have heartily approved of the Organisation's now famous motto as well, as no doubt, its aims and objectives.

Where Baden-Powell led the encircled British during the Siege of Mafeking, having to make use of local boys as runners, Popkess was in charge of the City of Nottingham and its civil defences prior to and during the Second World War. The latter was keen not to be under-prepared, and through his visits to Germany throughout the latter half of the 1930s (see chapter Sports) was well aware of the Nazi war plans. To this end, Popkess seized on his responsibilities and, as has been shown to be so typical of him, made them exemplary. Even as early as 1937, a full two years before its outbreak, The Captain was fully prepared in the event of war being declared. Nottingham's Air Raid Precautions were hailed as being the best in the country, with other area chiefs encouraged to visit Nottingham to view how their system was set up. By as early as September 1937, Popkess had plans in place for preservation of the City of Nottingham from the "menace from the air", which would comprise active roles for some 12,000 volunteers in roles from Air Raid Wardens to volunteer firefighters.

Popkess also commissioned detailed aerial maps of the City which had been produced by the RAF photographing it from an altitude of 6,000 feet, showing every street and alleyway. This was yet another example of Popkess' prudent efficiency in line with his radio development. By having the RAF produce it cost the City Police nothing, where an aerial survey firm would have charged over £300 at the time. These maps also showed the extensive system of information centres, volunteer co-ordination posts, and the five decontamination centres.[58]

So well-prepared were Popkess and Nottingham for enemy air raids that a ten-minute informational video was commissioned in 1938, highlighting Nottingham's defences and demonstrating an air raid drill. This video is still available on the British Film Institute website to view for free, and features Popkess giving out instructions. Moreover, it also gives an fantastic insight into the City of Nottingham at the time.[59]

Nottingham was far more prepared than even London, with Popkess making use of the city's extensive cave network, expanding and reinforcing the natural ready-made air raid shelters across the city area. One of the largest of these shelters was directly underneath Central Police Station on Shakespeare Street in the heart of the City, with the entrance right by the back

58 *Nottingham Evening Post*, 6th September 1937 p.5
59 Available at player.bfi.org.uk/free/film/watch-arp-a-practical-demonstration-of-nottingham-precautions-1938-online as accessed February 2018.

door of the station itself. Central Police and Fire Station (the Fire Service was a sub-division of the police at the time) was only opened in 1938, and it is entirely conceivable that as part of the construction process, with his penchant for planning and preparation, Popkess had insisted on the incorporation of the large air raid shelter underneath. Certainly, he had been visiting Nazi Germany for several years prior, and would have been very familiar with their ultra-militaristic imperial philosophy. He had also observed the effects of aerial bombing during the Spanish Civil War 1936-39.

The Central Police Station two-storey air raid shelter also accommodated the ARP control centre as well as the police and fire control centres,[60] and such was its success that it is still fully navigable to this day. Furthermore, until the police and fire services moved out the building in 2016 it was still used by the fire service for training, with the caverns being filled with smoke. This, in spite of the adjacent University building taking a direct hit from a German bomb.[61]

Popkess' air raid precautions were not solely reliant on the use of Nottingham's famous caves; they were far more pro-active and integrated than that. There were some 288 shelters in Nottingham City which provided accommodation for 33,200 people, of which the caves only accounted for 7,754. The remainder were provided by basements in public buildings and shops, and some surface shelters. Some 24,200 families on the city's housing estates were issued with Anderson shelters, and basements in 6,400 houses

60 Needham, David" *Battle of the Flames: Nottinghamshire's fight for survival in WWII Ashbourne*, Derbyshire: The Horizon Press 2009 p. 7
61 nfs-afs.org.uk/2014/04/09/tour-of-nottingham-central-fire-station-and-blitz-locations as accessed February 2018

were strengthened.[62]

Popkess was not content to allow his adopted home town to simply burn above ground whilst its inhabitants were safely ensconced underground, even if he did describe some of parts of the city as some of the worst slums in this country.[63] These slums can be seen in the aforementioned ARP demonstration film which takes place around the city's Broad Marsh area. Nottingham's air raid precautions and response therefore comprised a fully-integrated system of ARP wardens, full-time and special Constables, rapid-response fire-fighting vehicles and fire-fighters, air raid sirens, medical personnel and the shelters all combining to form a well-oiled machine.

The informational film from 1938 demonstrates this inter-connectivity and is worth describing. It perfectly demonstrates the high level of organisation and planning which Popkess had undertaken, which was typical of all his endeavours, and shows the degree of thought to which he put his mind.

The air raid drill begins with Popkess in full police uniform tunic and hat reading out some form of notice through a microphone, watched by crowds of onlookers. Sadly the film has no sound (audio still being in relative infancy in films, especially outside of a studio environment), but a helpful flash card tells us that this notice is an 'outline of the proceedings'. As he is reading, it is immediately clear that the drill is not confined to a sterile training area such as a military base or similar, but is taking part in the heart of Nottingham City Centre. This must have been intentional on the part of Popkess, in order that the civilian inhabitants of

62 Needham: *Battle of the Flames* p. 7
63 Popkess, Athelstan: *Nottingham City Police Centenary 1935* Nottingham: Nottingham City Police Press (1945) pp. 24-5.

Popkess reads out instructions for the Air Raid drill

the city were also fully involved, so they too could be prepared for the possible horrors of aerial bombardment.

Viewers are then shown some of the city's other integrated ARP resources, with casually-dressed men walking the streets sporting 'ARP warden' armbands and large wooden clackers, a black car with two men in the front sporting the registration plate 'ARP 2', and a unit of men marching in step with 'special constable' armbands on. Suddenly it cuts to a large air whistle on the side of a building which visibly sounds, and a flash card proclaiming "take cover!" is displayed. A six-strong squadron of bi-planes then flies over, obviously representing the enemy bombers. Clearly, Popkess had wanted to make the role-play scenario as realistic as he possibly could, and had enlisted the assistance of the Royal Air Force with some of its more out-dated aircraft to participate.

An explosion is then seen in an already largely demolished building, with the large crowds visible in the background kept at a safe distance behind large wooden barriers. Another flash card then states "The next Patrol Car Pump is immediately put into action". The black car seen before arrives, now towing a fire-fighting trailer, and a team of police firefighters unhitch it and take a ladder off it. This is erected against the side of the building, and one rescuer ascends, to retrieve a 'wounded person' from the 2nd floor. Meanwhile one team connects the trailer to the water mains and another team of police firefighters sees to the casualty. By now the building is well ablaze, and additional pumps are sent for, along with a 'fire float' – a barge on the nearby city canal fitted with long hoses and a large pump. Fire fighters run the hoses out to the scene of the fire as more car-towed pumps and a proper fire engine arrive at the scene.

Meanwhile, the 'enemy aircraft' continue to buzz overhead and another flash card tells us that "Sightseeing 'Nosey Parkers' are quickly Machine Gunned"! Several apparent 'civilians' are then seen to suffer some very ham-acting injuries ostensibly at the hands of the enemy aircraft machine guns, whilst ARP wardens usher others away to safety. These 'casualties' are then bandaged and taken away in police ambulances (both the ambulance service and the fire service in Nottingham at this time were branches of the police).

The aircraft then return again 'with mustard gas' and all the role-players don gas masks and signs are put out declaring

"Danger Gas". The City Council cleansing department are then put to work with their large street cleaning lorries dousing the roadways with water which is then brushed away by the various personnel before sand is spread over the area in a move to decontaminate it. The house 'hit by the bombs', now no longer ablaze, is then demolished by a demolition squad, so as not to be a collapse hazard.

The whole action is detailed in order to show the in-depth lengths and extent of planning involved in the drill, which was clearly designed to cover as many different scenarios as possible. This level of planning was absolutely typical of Popkess, and this demonstration film is perhaps the easiest means to convey this, especially in such a relatively short visual format. Popkess was in charge of Nottingham's air raid precautions and, as such, the idea behind organising and involving all the different elements in the drill would most likely have been his. This extensive planning and preparation, even a year before war had been declared, demonstrates that Popkess was markedly ahead of the curve, especially when even many people in power, including the Prime Minister Neville Chamberlain, were in significant denial about the prospect of it. It is easy, when watching this film, to see why Nottingham's preparations were hailed as an example to be followed nationally.

As it transpired, Nottingham was not targeted by the Luftwaffe to anywhere near the same degree as other core cities or military targets. Almost certainly, however, the degree of preparation and planning led by Popkess saved many lives in the city on the occasions the bombs did fall.

***

The Captain did not limit his war preparations to the Second World War. 'Peace' under its true definition did not follow that awful six years. Instead, the world was plunged into the constant all-pervasive fear of Nuclear Apocalypse during the Cold War. Whilst not as familiar with the Russian Soviets as he was with the German Nazis, Popkess again did not rest on his laurels, and continued to make sure that his adopted home was fully prepared in the event of an outbreak of war, or even a nuclear strike. To this end he led the planning against this eventuality, as he had with the pre-War Air Raid Precautions.

Making full use of new and improving technologies, on 14th May 1956 Popkess organised a Civil Defence drill day. This incorporated various police resources in innovative new ways to cover scenarios in the event of the city being devastated by a nuclear bomb, or the case of Soviet invasion. A team of five officers and two police dogs took to the skies in a helicopter over the city. They were initially tasked with guiding a 'civil defence column' of rescuers and medics through Nottingham from the air, represented in the drill by a police radio van. This was done by Inspector Bonser using a police radio to direct the van through streets, which in the scenario were blocked by rubble, collapsing buildings and fleeing people. Neither the van crew nor the helicopter crew knew each other's plans, as they wouldn't in reality, and the helicopter crew had to first locate the van, only being told it was heading from the north of the county. They did this, and then Inspector Bonser directed it through the streets into the city centre, under the watch of Supt Watson who was leading the operation.

After the completion of this scenario the helicopter team took off again and were tasked with a dog training exercise. In this drill the helicopter flew from the south to the east of the city, landing at Colwick Racecourse where the two dogs and their handlers were dropped off and tasked to locate a man hiding there. This exercise was in part to simulate an urgent response to enemy parachutists, and also to train the dogs to help look for people lost in more rural areas.

Not one to waste the special resource that had been arranged for the day, Popkess, his Assistant Chief Constable of the time F. Porter and Alderman Coffey, then vice chair of the Watch Committee (and whom shall be encountered later during The Popkess Affair), also took to the sky on four additional helicopter flights. These were used by the senior officers and others on board to study the city's traffic problems from the air, to aid their understanding with regards to improving traffic flow and help underpin his work around improving that, as was seen in the chapter Road Traffic.[64]

***

As demonstrated by all the time spent on his innovations, planning, operational matters and sporting events (as shall be seen in the next chapter), Popkess was a very busy man. It was clear that Nottingham City Police was his life, and it seems probable that this passion for the job resulted in his divorce from his first wife Gilberta in the mid-late 1930s.

In the summer of 1918, Athelstan Popkess had wed Gilberta Lillian Popkiss, a nurse, in Thanet, Kent. It doesn't take much to work out how Popkess, at that time convalescing and recovering from his various Tropical fevers contracted during the War, got talking to a young nurse whom, it so happened, shared his

---

64 *Nottingham Evening Post*, 15th May 1956 in Hyndman, PC David: *Nottingham City Police: A Pictorial History 1930–1960* p. 39

surname (albeit with an 'i' not an 'e'). Such was the confusion over them having the same surname that in the marriage record both are recorded as being called Popkiss, before and after the ceremony.

Gilberta and Athelstan had two children, Virginia Cherrie, who was born in the summer of 1931, and Richard Simon, who was born on 4th March 1933. Given the feverous pace at which Popkess was working on his wireless communications and Mechanized Division at this time, opening the new Forensic Laboratory and his European tour of those already established, all the other initiatives progressing in the pipeline and the actual business of leading a police force, it must be the case that he was spending too much time away when Gilberta was at home raising two young children.

Dennis Silverwood recalls how Popkess even had an ante-room adjoining his office at the City Police Headquarters that had a bed in it. Popkess would retire there regularly after working late into the night on various initiatives or projects. How long Popkess had been using this room when Silverwood joined him in 1953 is not clear, but it must have been some length of time, with him regularly working late into the night and unwilling to face the journey home before he made the decision to introduce it.

The demands on Gilberta being almost a single mother to two small children and coming a clear second-place to her husband's job must have caused a lot of discord, ultimately ending in her leaving him. Such was Popkess' dedication to the job, as evidenced by his need for a bedroom off his office and making sure that Nottingham City Police led the field in as many areas as possible, that he lost his young family because of it. It would seem that Popkess was more concerned with his physical legacy in the

City Police than he was his biological one, although it transpired that the apple didn't fall too far from the tree, with his daughter ending up retiring as a Superintendent in the Sussex Police Force.

Popkess remarried only a few years later, in March 1939, when he wed Dorothy Rosemary Walsh in Nottingham. The new Mrs Popkess put up with her husband's work ethic longer than Gilberta did, but this marriage too was to end in sadness and controversy.

It is clear that his work meant everything to Popkess, and this is yet another reason why it is a shame that he is not better remembered to the history of British Policing, considering all that he gave and lost for it. His intense passion for the job would ultimately cost him two wives, his mental health and the job itself, as will be seen in the chapter on The Popkess Affair.

There was another passion in Popkess' life, however, one that ran concurrently to his passion for policing and that went hand-in-hand with it. It was a passion that bolstered his desires to have a workforce at the peak of fitness and abilities. That passion was Sport, and it is to that hobby that the next chapter is devoted.

8.

SPORTS

Since the time of his youth Popkess had always been a keen sportsman. Growing up in South Africa and Rhodesia in the days before televisions or radios, children would spend their time playing outdoors. Much of this time, especially for active, rugged children such as Popkess, would have been spent playing sports. Rugby is the national sport of South Africa, and certainly Popkess was no stranger to the game.

Such were his abilities at rugby that he claims on his application for the Chief Constable position to have played for his country against England in 1913.[65] The team of his birth country, the South African Springboks, did tour Great Britain over the winter of 1912-13 and played England on 4th January 1913. Bizarrely, however, the team sheet from the time does not back up this assertion, with Popkess' name not appearing on the touring squad. His *Database of Notable Persons* entry suggests that Popkess played for the Rhodesian national team, but no records can be found of a Rhodesian side playing England in 1913. It would seem very unlikely for Popkess to have lied on his

---

65 The National Archives HO 45/24711 City of Nottingham Appointment of Chief Constable Form of Application 'Athelstan Popkess'

121

formal application, especially about something so irrelevant to the position applied for and given his clear penchant for honesty and integrity. Casting further doubt on the claim, however, is that Popkess would have only just been approaching his 19th birthday when the tour began in October 1912. Whilst not necessarily young for an international rugby player today, it was very much so at that time. Quite why Popkess would make this claim on his application that appears to be false cannot be known. It would not even be the case that he could have represented the South African military versus English armed forces, because as seen on page 14, Popkess did not sign up until 1914 following the outbreak of War.

The other sporting claim he makes on his application is that of being a "Qualified Boxing Referee and Judge." There can be no doubt as to the veracity of this statement. Boxing was a clear and undeniable passion for The Captain, and he was to make no efforts to hide this throughout his leadership tenure. Former PC Bob Rosamund recalls how gifted boxers were shown significant favour by Popkess, one example being that members of the force boxing team could have as much time away from duties as they liked to practice their sparring. Another case of rules being bent to accommodate those handy with their fists and feet is that of PC 'Killer' Lewis. Recruited into the force at the time when the minimum height for male recruits was 5' 7", not to mention Popkess' significant bias towards those of an even taller disposition, Lewis was only 5' 4" tall. Crucially though he was a highly-accomplished boxer, who went on to win the International Police Boxing Championship in the middleweight category in 1936.[66]

---

66 Hyndman, PC David: *Nottingham City Police: A Pictorial History 1930–1960* p.15

His devotion to boxing, and the fostering of the Nottingham City Police boxing team, was perhaps the only distraction from his innovating and overseeing of the force that Popkess allowed himself. It was perhaps the only 'holiday' that he took as well. Popkess encouraged friendly rivalries between the Nottingham City team and other police teams, most notably the Stuttgart Police team in Germany. Several reciprocal visits were arranged between Nottingham and Stuttgart, with Popkess accompanying his fighters to continental Europe. These visits, occurring as they did in the mid-to-late 1930s when Germany was in the full throws of Nazification, did cause issues for The Captain, as was seen in the chapter Controversies. The Nottingham City Police team of the 1930s were, however, "considered to be the best amateur boxing team in Europe... [producing] several International and A.B.A. Champions at various weights".[67]

So proud was he of the force's sporting achievements that Popkess chose to conclude his celebration of the Centenary of Nottingham City Police booklet by writing about the force's sporting prowess. This booklet, transcribed from a paper he gave to the Nottingham Thoroton Society in April 1945, details the 100-year history of the Nottingham City Force, its trials and tribulations. Popkess finished this speech by writing:

"In the direction of sport too, the Force has not been exactly un-distinguished. During the past twelve years, for instance, it has succeeded in winning no fewer than fourteen International Police Boxing Championships. Its members have numbered too, three Welsh, three English, and two Scottish A.B.A Boxing champions. As well as two British Empire Games representatives. It has also produced an Olympic Games

67 Ibid. p. 11

representative in wrestling, the only wrestler in this country who ever succeeded in winning the Middle Weight, Light-Heavy Weight, and Heavy Weight Championships of England in the same year.

As to cricket, without wishing to seem too optimistic, it may not be overstating the case to say that the City Police Cricket First Eleven before the war, was capable of giving many Minor County Elevens a good bending. One young Constable has recently opened the batting for England; another, a left arm slow bowler, has on occasions played with the distinction for the County side; and of course other members of the Force have played in the County Eleven from time to time. Members of the Force won the Life Saving Team Championship of the British Police in 1934."[68]

It is also clear from the above passage the national nature of the make-up of the staff in the Force at the time. Popkess highlights the Welsh, Scottish and English boxing champions, and it can be assumed that those men were most likely approached directly by the Chief to work in the City Police based on their existing boxing skills.

Popkess' passion for sports was also not limited to those he played. His support for physical exercise ran to all sports, with the Nottingham City Police boasting teams or participants in a spectrum ranging through swimming, athletics, life-saving, football, cricket, hockey and tug-of-war! Included in this list were footballers who played for Nottinghamshire County football club, national wrestling champions who represented Great Britain at the Olympic Games, and international cricketers.[69] Almost all the Force's teams or individual competitors won national police

68 Popkess, Athelstan: *Nottingham City Police Centenary 1935* pp. 25-26
69 Popkess, Athelstan: *Nottingham City Police Centenary 1935*. Passim

championships in their respective fields regularly. Whilst this sporting legacy diminished steadily after Popkess' retirement, there were to be occasional further successes for Nottinghamshire Police officers in sports. Most notable of these was a young PC Christopher Dean, who (when paired with a certain Jayne Torvill) won a memorable Olympic Gold medal at figure skating.

Such was Popkess' passion for all things sport that he authorised the purchase by the Force of a large piece of land off Mansfield Road in the Sherwood area of the City to be used as police sports ground. Complete with running track, football/rugby pitch and athletics field, an annual Nottingham City Police sports day was held there, as well as hosting the various teams' activities and training sessions. This land sadly now has housing on it, its days as a sports and training ground for police officers long gone.

Not content with simply encouraging proficient sportsmen (and it was almost exclusively men) to both join and develop their abilities in the Force, officers were required as part of their employment conditions to undertake regular sporting activities, even in their own time. Rose Hall, a Police Woman in Nottingham City Police between 1954 and 1963, recalls how a superintendent in the late 1950s ordered all his officers to attend the City's Victoria Baths for swimming practice every Sunday morning, in which she was paired with PC Dennis 'Tug' Wilson.[70]

There is a strong case to be made here again for Popkess being head of the curve in this field also. The physical attributes of a constable can, *in extremis*, make all the difference in successfully detaining a criminal or mourning the death of an officer, even more so at the time of Popkess' stewardship when 'Personal

70 Phillips, Robert & Andrews, Tom: *100 Years of Women in Policing Nottingham:* Nottinghamshire Police (2015).

Protective Equipment' consisted of essentially a wooden stick and a whistle. In the 21st Century officers have body armour, CS or Pepper Spray, Taser, extendable batons and personal radios that can summon assistance at great speed in vehicles. Even so, it is recognised that there is still a need for an annual fitness test to ensure that officers are physically able to undertake their duties. Popkess was essentially ensuring this was the case, some 80 years before the fitness tests became mandatory in England.

Popkess' desire for his officers to participate in sports, especially those such as boxing, rugby and wrestling, ensured that those officers were 'tough'. The lack of ability to call for back-up when patrolling beat areas on foot alone, especially in some rougher areas such as Nottingham's Narrow Marsh district, meant that officers would have to resolve often violent and dangerous situations on their own. This feeds back into Professor Clive Emsley's theory about 'tough coppers', where the officer patrolling notoriously rough districts needed to be 'harder' than those he was policing in order to both command respect and ensure his safety and that of others.[71] Being a British boxing champion or Olympic wrestler almost certainly ensured that status.

What is up for debate, however, is the cost versus benefit of the sporting focus; whether the number of officer hours lost from front-line policing to training was worth the benefit of additional fitness and toughness. Clearly, in today's police force the balance has swung fully the other way, with almost all sporting activity required to be undertaken in officers' personal time.

There were also associated benefits to Nottingham City Police

---

71 Emsley, Clive: *The English and Violence since 1750* Hambledon and London: London (2005).

at the time, however. The national and international prestige and public relations benefits to the force, as evidenced by PC Bob Rosamund, who moved from London to specifically join Nottingham City Police over any other; the international relations and the associated knowledge of war preparations fostered by the visits to Germany, and the respect of the population of Nottingham to its police force who represented them not just locally, but internationally at sports. Were these benefits worth the lost policing time? Certainly, in today's media and political climate such abstractions would be very controversial indeed, but at the time of Popkess it certainly appears from his standing amongst the people of Nottingham that they heartily approved of his policy.

This standing amongst the people of Nottingham was to prove a significant help at the very end of his career, when Popkess was attacked by politicians seeking to undermine and discredit him. The support of the local people ensured that this matter garnered national attention and infamy. It is this Affair to which the next chapter turns.

9.

THE POPKESS AFFAIR

The Popkess Affair is the incident for which its eponymous protagonist is best and almost solely-remembered to the history of policing. It also brought Captain Popkess to national attention in 1959, when it hit headlines in news media of the time and resulted in the intercession on his behalf by not only the Home Secretary, but also by around 6,000 Nottingham residents demonstrating in the city's Market Square. A direct result of this one man's determination not to back down in the sure-fire knowledge of his cause, along with a couple of unrelated, less prestigious (or perhaps less notorious) incidents in other forces, led directly to a Royal Commission into policing. This in turn defined the place of policing with regards to politics and local government. It ultimately led to the removal of direct political interference or control of policing for over half a century, from 1959 until the introduction of politically-elected Police and Crime Commissioners in 2012.

A thoroughly comprehensive summary of the entirety of the events entitled "Politicians and the Police in Nottingham: The Popkess Affair" was published in the Nottinghamshire history journal *Transactions of the Thoroton Society of Nottinghamshire*, Vol 108, 2004. written by one of Popkess' Chief Superintendents,

Alfred S Bowley, following his retirement.

It is from this excellent article that this chapter largely derives, and it would be almost impossible to describe the events of it in detail without simply plagiarising Bowley's account. Bowley researched the matter extensively, as well as having worked through it at the time in the Nottingham City Police. He looks at both the viewpoints of Capt Popkess and the police, as well as the Labour Council of the time. He does a good job drawing on multiple contemporary sources and archived documents to write a detailed account of events.

Whilst Bowley primarily tells Popkess' side of the story, the account of his supposed adversaries in the City's Labour Party is detailed by Nick Hayes in a chapter of his book *Consensus and Controversy: City Politics in Nottingham 1945-1966*. Hayes draws extensively on minutes from Nottingham Corporation[72] and Watch Committee meetings as well as private correspondence between the politicians to piece together the viewpoints of the key protagonists in the Council who were opposed to Popkess' actions which sparked the scandal. Whilst perhaps less biased to either 'side' than Bowley's account, Hayes does seem to err in favour of the Labour group regarding the Affair, albeit he is notably critical of their policy of secrecy and trying to simply bury the matter and hope that it would "lie down and die of its own accord".

Both accounts are equally insightful; Bowley's for an overarching, easy-to-read account broadly detailing the facts of the Affair, and Hayes' for a deeper, more academic insight into the

---

72   The elected governing body of the City at the time was referred to as the 'Nottingham Corporation', but is now known as the Nottingham City Council. I will primarily use the latter term for familiarity.

political background and reasons behind how it came to happen.

**

Taken at face value, the root cause of the Popkess Affair is the alleged bribing of Nottingham City Councillors by a company seeking to build, of all things, a planetarium in the city. Saying this, however, is akin to attributing the First World War to the assassination of Archduke Franz Ferdinand. The reality of the situation is, as would be expected, far more complicated, and boils down to a power struggle between several strong-willed, stubborn individuals in positions of authority.

The two key protagonists in the narrative are the eponymous Capt Popkess, whose role was to investigate allegations of criminality in whatever guise that may be. His 'adversary' was Tom Owen, Town Clerk of Nottingham Corporation: the City's chief legal officer and a former police prosecuting solicitor. Both men had a key supporter within the Council. For Popkess this was the Labour chairperson of the Watch Committee Chris Coffey, and for Owen was Alderman George Wigman, leader of the City Council and its finance committee. All four men held senior positions and, it would appear, strongly disliked being told how to do their job by others.

The Popkess Affair began in 1958 when a German company conducted a scoping exercise with regards to the possibility of building a planetarium in Nottingham. Representatives of the German scientific and optical company initially wrote to the council, and after a brief correspondence with Tom Owen over the costs and potential incomes, wherein it was established that the total would be £150,000 plus staffing costs with minimal income opportunities (over £2.5m today), the idea was rejected. The company's local agent, however, had connections in parliament, and using these arranged for Alderman Wigman along with another council member and the Labour Council secretary to attend the company's headquarters in Germany at the company's expense. There they were entertained with demonstrations of the planetarium and given cameras made by the firm as gifts.

Upon their return to Nottingham in November 1958 Alderman Wigman chaired a meeting at which the press were to quote him as saying that the purchase of a planetarium was "a must", although he later denied saying this.[73] At a meeting of the City Council on 5th January 1959 a Conservative councillor was asked who was covering the costs of the trip to Germany, to which Alderman Wigman replied that he had covered the expenses himself.[74]

Crucially, the planetarium firm was located in East Germany, which in 1958/59 was at the height of the Cold War. (For context, the Berlin Airlift was only nine years previously, the Berlin Wall would be built two years later, and the Cuban Missile Crisis still four years in the future.) Naturally, a visit by three Socialist Labour Party councillors into Communist East Germany at the time was a matter for gossip and speculation. It was this gossip, linked with the issue of the expenses and the gratuities received (as well as possibly the concern over a Communist East German firm potentially being paid vast sums of British Pounds by a left-wing Council) that was to kick off the Popkess Affair.

The day after the expenses question, on 6th January 1959, a prospective Liberal MP living in Nottingham called Stanley Thomas wrote to Capt Popkess stating:

73 *Nottingham Guardian Journal*, 10th December 1958 p.1
74 *Nottingham Evening Post*, 6th January 1959 p.7

"I would be grateful if you would take notice of certain rumours going round the city regarding the visit of certain city Councillors to Germany recently."[75]

Having received the letter, which whilst not making direct allegations certainly cast aspersions on the actions of the three Council members, Popkess forwarded it on to the Metropolitan Police requesting they investigate. He asked that the nature of this investigation focussed on ascertaining who had invited the trio to East Germany and paid their travel and sundry expenses, as well as looking into the nature of the gratuities they received.

While this investigation was being conducted by the Met, town clerk Tom Owen was instructed by Alderman Wigman to find a site for the possible planetarium and also arrange for members of the Council to visit the existing one in London, which 27 Councillors duly did.

In this same month of January 1959 in which Alderman Wigman and his cronies were actively looking at spending £150,000 on a planetarium already demonstrated by Owen to be a white elephant, Popkess and his main proponent in the Council and chair of the Watch Committee, Alderman Coffey, took their Traffic Warden proposal to the Finance Committee, which was chaired by Wigman. They were told there was no money for it. Apparently on the advice of Owen, the Finance Committee similarly rejected an already heavily watered-down plea by Popkess and Coffey for additional police housing in the city, of which there was a desperate shortage. This led to a significant fall-out between Coffey and Wigman, with Coffey publicly calling

---

75 Nottinghamshire Archives Account Number 6196 Letter from Stanley Thomas to the Chief Constable 6th January 1959

out Wigman over the Planetarium.[76]

This fall-out and railing against the leader of the Council, who appears to have led in a somewhat autocratic manner and whom Nottingham historian Nick Hayes describes as having "Incestuous hierarchical control over policy making at the time", led to Coffey being requested to resign from the Watch Committee, which he refused, and then being expelled from the local Labour party.[77]

The planetarium dispute continued, with Stanley Thomas the 'letter writer' continuing to press Popkess for updates. These were duly received by him at the end of January, with the Metropolitan Police outlining that the Councillors had declared the cameras to Customs and Alderman Wigman paying the required duty on them himself.

A further letter on 12th February stated that the planetarium company's UK agents had paid the airfare, and the company itself the hotel and sundry expenses in East Germany. This should perhaps have marked the end of the investigation, but Thomas was not satisfied with Popkess' responses – most likely as he saw a political weakness to exploit and wished to hammer it home. On 2nd April he again wrote to Popkess, ostensibly saying that if the Nottingham City Police would not take the matter seriously he would go to the Home Secretary directly. With a huge dose of irony, potentially out of a desire not to turn the matter into such a fuss, Popkess sought the advice of the Director of Public Prosecutions (DPP) on whether there were in fact any issues to investigate under the Public Bodies Corrupt Practices Act 1889 (Corruption in Office).

---

76 Hayes, Nick: *Consensus and Controversy: City Politics in Nottingham 1945-1966* Liverpool: Liverpool University Press (1996) pp. 139-140
77 Ibid.

In a typed four-page letter dated 3rd April 1959 Pokess wrote to the DPP outlining the circumstances of the case as he saw them, detailing how he felt Alderman Wigman and Councillor Butler had misled the Council over the planetarium, having at no time declared their trip to Germany on the account of the planetarium company. Popkess also quoted Wigman's statement of the purchase being "a must", and highlighted the issues of the lack of prior agreement for the Germany trip on the part of the general Council or any committee, the receiving of gifts by the three travellers, and the question of any expenses incurred and who was covering them – specifically them being paid by the planetarium company. Finally, he referenced the Scotland Yard investigation, which had been told by the planetarium company's UK agents that Nottingham's proposed purchase had been deferred, before the matter had even been discussed in any Council meeting and that conclusion reached.[78]

Reading between the lines of the letter, Popkess was alleging that essentially the entire planetarium proposal was a vanity project of Alderman Wigman, who had taken advantage of an all-expenses paid trip to Germany (and another a month later to London) with his friends (one of whom wasn't even on the Council), and all received a free gift of an expensive camera; hyped up the project to the Council, and upon becoming the subject of scrutiny in the Council chamber and the press had kyboshed the whole thing saying there was no money for it.

Popkess' letter strongly conveys the view that the entire planetarium idea had only really ever been tangible in the mind of Alderman Wigman, who had used it for the personal gain of him and his cronies.

78 National Archives 272/83 Letter from Popkess to DPP 3rd April 1959

He was duly advised by the chief prosecutor to conduct an investigation into possible corruption in a public office, writing:

"The subsequent conduct of these Council members and their lack of frankness with the City Council inevitably raises a doubt as to their bona fides and, in my opinion justifies further police enquiries."[79]

This entirely justified the subsequent continuation of enquiries by Popkess into possible wrongdoing on the part of the Councillors; the most senior prosecutor in the country giving the opinion that they should be conducted. Popkess again referred the matter to Scotland Yard, and this time two detectives journeyed to Nottingham and conducted investigations between 22nd April and 12th May 1959. The presence of the Scotland Yard detectives investigating the Council hit the local press on 6th May – a day prior to local municipal elections. It was this significant timing of the information leak that has seemingly ignited the fire of the Council against Popkess, with Alderman Wigman later quoted as saying:

"The reports could only have come from inside local police circles... Scotland Yard has denied having anything to do with the release of this information... As only a limited number of people in the City Police had this information, one doesn't have to look too far to know where it came from."[80]

This statement was published in the *Nottingham Evening Post* on 19th August, only a week after Popkess had been re-instated following his suspension over the Affair, so it is not too much of a

---

79 Hayes: *Consensus and Controversy* p.142
80 *Nottingham Evening Post*, 19th August 1959

leap of faith to conclude that Wigman held Popkess responsible for the information disclosure.

It was in fact not Popkess who leaked the presence of the detectives and the investigation into alleged malfeasance by Wigman, however. In his comprehensive narrative of the Affair, Alfred Bowley writes how in 2004 he spoke to the journalist responsible for breaking the story. Bowley had it disclosed to him that it was in fact a senior Council member who had passed the information on, following a meeting of the Council in which the investigation was raised.

This information came out neither at the time nor in the subsequent inquiry during Popkess' suspension, nor during the Royal Commission hearings. It has taken until 2004 to clear Popkess' name from this suggestion, but in May 1959 the reputational damage had been done to Popkess in the eyes of Wigman and his allies.

This was compounded by a further investigation requested by Popkess and conducted simultaneously by the Scotland Yard officers into further alleged misconduct by Alderman Wigman. A question had been asked by the same journalist responsible for the investigation disclosure to Alderman Coffey of all people about a rumour he had heard that Wigman had used City Council labour and resources to construct a driveway at his personal home. Coffey, no doubt still embittered by his treatment at the hands of Wigman regarding his actions on the Watch Committee, passed this information on to Capt Popkess, requesting he investigate. This investigation showed that some £25 of materials (£400 today) had been invoiced for delivery and work at one address, but was in fact being installed at a different address - which was Wigman's own private home. There were also four labourers and a supervisor involved in the work for the day. Wigman claimed to have paid for the materials and labour, but the receipts he produced to the detectives did not correlate to the invoices.

With Wigman already turned against Popkess due to his presumption that The Captain had leaked the investigation into the planetarium, it was now Owen's turn to take umbrage at the City's Chief of Police. The investigations into Wigman's drive needed copies of invoices and other paperwork from the Council but Owen refused access to them, arguing that he felt the issue of any impropriety on the part of Wigman over his driveway was wholly an internal misconduct matter. He wrote to Popkess that he would investigate, and if he concluded there were any criminal matters he would pass the relevant material to the police.

Owen does not mince his words in this letter, openly stating he feels Popkess is biased and bent on bringing down the Council:

> "I have already told you that I will consult you if I decide that it is necessary to employ the Police for a prosecution. Your way of dealing with this investigation, with the investigation about the Planetarium and with the investigation about claims by members of the Council for loss of earnings has made it impossible for me to do anything with you about matters of this kind. I take a very serious view of what you have done in these matters to the denigration of the City Council and its members but I have decided that as you have only a few months to serve before retirement I will do nothing about your methods."[81]

It is clear that by this stage any suggestion of co-operation

---

81 Nottinghamshire Archives Account 6196 Letter from Town Clerk to Chief Constable 3rd June 1959.

and respect between Popkess and Owen/Wigman had gone, and both sides clearly believed the other was waging a concerted smear and obfuscation campaign against them. On this same day, 3rd June, Popkess received a letter from the DPP stating that upon reviewing the evidence from the Scotland Yard detectives, whatever ones opinion with regards to the actions of Wigman et al, their conduct was not criminal in nature.

On the same day the Watch Committee met to demand an explanation from both Popkess and Owen as to how the planetarium investigation had come about. A series of terse correspondence between Popkess and Owen ensued, in which Popkess was asked by Owen to disclose all material relating to the investigation to the Watch Committee. Popkess replied asking why, and what would be done with the information which was sensitive police documentation. Owen responded that he was of the opinion that the Chief Constable was obliged to divulge the information as it related to the City Council, whom Owen saw as Popkess' employers and masters.

Popkess refused to provide this information to Owen, seemingly based on his beliefs that the documents represented sensitive police information on a key official, much of which had already been leaked. To draw a perhaps hyperbolic comparison, it would be akin to providing details of a murder inquiry to the suspect's family and friends. It may also be partly that Popkess felt that because Owen was refusing to release documents he had requested into Wigman's driveway inquiry, Popkess would play the same game.

In any event, a month later, on 8th July, the Watch Committee met, attended by Popkess and his deputy Chief Constable as well as Owen. The Committee again requested the documents pertaining to the planetarium enquiry from the Chief Constable, who maintained his stated position that the Watch Committee were not entitled to them and the police could refuse to make public any aspect of any police inquiry. Interestingly, and perhaps a key reason for Popkess' refusal to divulge details of the investigation, was that both Alderman Wigman and Cllr. Butler, who had travelled to East Germany with him, were present and participated in the meeting.

Owen diametrically opposed this viewpoint, arguing variously that the Committee was legally entitled to receive a report from its Chief Constable; that he felt Popkess' belligerence, and the root cause of the supposed vendetta against Wigman stemmed from the refusal of the finance committee to fund the Traffic Wardens proposal and the police housing; and also expressed his concern over Popkess' conduct during the investigations. He furthermore added that he felt none of the investigations should have ever been conducted by the police, but internally by the Council.[82]

The Chief Constable and his deputy were asked to leave the room by the majority Labour Watch Committee, and upon their return Popkess was informed that he was suspended from duty with immediate effect. The following day the grounds for this were issued to Popkess in writing by none other than Owen, these being:

1) The Chief Constable's refusal to comply with the committee's instruction to inform the committee about the inquiries by Scotland Yard officers into corporation matters in Nottingham.

2) The report by the Town Clerk of the Chief Constable's conduct.

---

82 Nottingham City Council Watch Committee minutes 8th July 1959

3) The Chief Constable's statement that he intended to ask for a public enquiry.[83]

The case of the Nottingham Chief Constable investigating supposed corruption in his local council who had then suspended him from duty had now made national press and drawn unwanted attention to the City Councillors on a national scale. Not least because the reasons for the suspension were not made public until 5th August, meaning the City Council were also accused of secrecy over the whole matter, making it appear even more under-handed.[84]

Popkess was able to have an open letter to Wigman and Butler published in *The Times* on 11th July 1959, in which he outlined his course of action and specific involvement of non-local detectives working primarily in London so as to intentionally not draw attention to the investigation and have it conducted impartially.[85] Such was the furore around the proceedings that the Home Secretary 'Rab' Butler became involved, writing to the key protagonists in the Council demanding explanations and hoping that the matter would be resolved quickly and expeditiously. Crucially, he made his stance known that he felt Popkess was correct in refusing to release details of the investigation to the Watch Committee, and essentially blackmailed the Watch Committee into re-instating Popkess by threatening to withhold the Home Office part of the City's police funding.

Meanwhile Stanley Thomas, perhaps feeling guilt at being the catalyst of the Affair, canvassed local businesses, out of which

83 Nottinghamshire Archives Account 6196 Letter from Town Clerk to Chief Constable 9th July 1959
84 Hayes *Consensus and Controversy* pp. 147-8
85 *The Times*, 11th July 1959 p.6

emerged a 6,000 signature-strong petition demanding Popkess' re-instatement. Like vultures circling a dying animal, the local Conservatives jumped bodily on the gathering bandwagon and organised a public rally in support of The Captain in the city's Market Square, directly in front of the Council House, on 20th July. Press reports of the time detail a 7,000 strong turnout chanting for Popkess' re-instatement and "justice for a great man". It was clear on which side public opinion had fallen.

Somehow the Labour party needed to save face, and it was clear after visits by Owen to see the Home Secretary that they were not going to 'win' the clash. It was therefore with reluctance that on 30th July the Watch Committee decided to re-instate Popkess, and he returned to work the following week on 10th August 1959.

The Committee left no doubt about their feelings on the matter however, recording as their official stance that

> "[The Watch Committee's] lack of confidence in the impartiality of the Chief Constable and having regard to the circumstances set out in this Resolution and to the fact that the Chief Constable is due to retire the Committee reluctantly reinstates him in office with effect from 9th August 1959."[86]

Popkess duly returned to office, walking back in to a pile of well-wishing correspondence four inches deep on his desk: a further indication of just which side public opinion had landed on. On his return, Popkess is reported to have described himself as a "prisoner in his own home" during his suspension.[87]

He was only to resume his duties for another four months,

---

86 Nottingham City Council Watch Committee Minutes 30th July 1959
87 *The Daily Telegraph*, 11th August 1959

before leaving Nottingham for retirement in December 1959. He was but a shadow of his former self, with former PC Dan Hyndman describing him as 'weary' in his book.[88] The fall-out of the Affair rumbled on for some time, with Alderman Wigman still publishing his views on the matter in local press a week after Popkess' return. This was most likely, on Wigman's part, a response to vehement and on-going press criticism of the local Labour Party and its handling of the situation, including the refusal to issue an apology or even appear sympathetic towards Popkess' position in its resolution of re-instatement.

The fallout from the Affair led to Alderman Wigman resigning his leadership of the Council shortly after Popkess' return; the reputational and political damage from the allegations against him which the Council had refused to allow be investigated, too much for even this autocrat to weather. In a twist of irony, in November 1959 Wigman's replacement invited none other than Alderman Coffey to chair an inquiry into the allegations against Wigman regarding the driveway at his house, and any other alleged improprieties in the Council. The police intervened, saying they were already investigating the matter and the Council duly handed over all the documents that Popkess had been requesting six months previously, as well as Owen's conclusions.

In that same month, the Watch Committee published a report into the Affair, which had been drafted by Owen. This report stopped short of directly accusing Popkess of having acted on malice, but Owen informed the Council that a lawyer had advised him that the report was defamatory towards Popkess and therefore should not be read outside of the Council and its

---

88   Hyndman, PC David: *Nottingham City Police: A Pictorial History 1930–1960* Newark: Davage Printing Ltd p. 75

legal privilege. This did not stop the report from being leaked, however, presumably by Coffey or a Conservative Councillor. Such was still the intense national interest in the matter that the report was published in the national *Daily Telegraph* on 25th November 1959 and in local press the following day.

What followed was finally a public debate on the matter in a full Council session, with the report forming the basis of the discussion. Hayes details from notes taken during the meeting how the city's Labour Party new-guard were keen to show transparency and some humility over the matter in order to put it behind them and move on. Only Owen and the Watch Committee members appeared to still be stuck-in-the-muds and continue to restate their position without remorse.

Coffey was also recorded as not pulling his punches in his scathing criticism of the Watch Committee and Owen and the secrecy with which they had conducted themselves. Apparently the only criticism levelled at Popkess during the debate was his failure to adequately co-operate with Owen, which had apparently been the case in the past in similar circumstances regarding the City and the Police. As has already been discussed, however, this failure to work harmoniously was a result of two big personalities both keen to assert their own authority and both markedly self-assured in their own beliefs.

What had started off as perhaps a relatively trivial matter had escalated due to this personality clash, and both protagonists entrenched belief in their own viewpoints. Bowley made no bones about blaming this downward spiral on Owens, writing that the clerk

"chose to ignore ... Home Office warnings. His letters to the Chief Constable became increasingly patronising, leaving a man of Popkess' disposition no possibility of compromise." [89]

In this last clause, Bowley could not have been more spot on. Popkess' entire background and personality was one of uncompromising command, discipline and respect, where he was used to having people follow his orders and respect his abilities. Put simply, Owen's tone would have been like a red rag to a bull. This does not however exonerate Popkess from his part in the descent of manners either.

Owen's convictions were also fundamentally flawed, in his belief that Popkess and the Nottingham City Police were a department of the Nottingham Corporation and thereby obliged to report to them. Whilst it was true that the large part of the police funding came from the local Council and were overseen and loosely directed by the Watch Committee, a stated court case from 1930 – *Fisher v Oldham Corporation* – had clearly defined constables (and therefore by extension the Chief Constable) as Crown Servants, not servants of the local authority. This meant that it was an already well-established precedent that Popkess was indeed not obliged to report to the Council on all matters that they requested, or follow any instructions issued by them which he felt was contrary to his duties as a police officer. Solicitors instructed by the Association of Chief Police Officers and the Nottingham Law Society independently reached the same conclusion.[90]

89 Bowley, Alfred S "Politicians and the Police in Nottingham: The Popkess Affair, 1959" in *Transactions of the Thoroton Society of Nottinghamshire* Vol. 108 (2004) p.184
90 Hull History Centre ACPO archives UDPO/10/918 Report to Association of Chief Police Officers by Messrs S Gerald Howard and Helenus Milmo 24th August 1959 and *The Daily Telegraph*, 7th August 1959.

Ultimately, the police, with the documents provided by the committee, reached the decision that there had indeed been improprieties on the part of both Wigman and the town engineer who had overseen the work at Wigman's house and who cross-invoiced the materials and labour. This investigation, however, was not concluded until 1960.

The case was passed to the Director of Public Prosecutions, who agreed with the findings. Their decision, however, was that there was likely insufficient evidence to convict either man, and that it was not in the public interest to bring prosecutions against either due to the events having taken place some three years prior and amounting to only £25. This decision was given to the Nottingham City Police on 11th March 1960, and with that ended public and press interest in The Popkess Affair.

The allegations by Owen and Wigman of bias on the part of Popkess do on the face of it appear to have some credibility, especially when set against the backdrop of the Traffic Wardens and police housing issues. It is important, however, to recognise the persistence of the initial 'letter writer' Stanley Thomas in instigating the planetarium and driveway investigations. Even at the outset, Popkess in his own words recognised a potential conflict of interests and straight away requested the Metropolitan Police to conduct the investigation as opposed to the Nottingham City Police. This may also be linked to the possible Communist subtext of the visit to East Germany by very left-wing politicians, and there is the possibility he requested some surreptitious enquiries be made by Special Branch alongside the more public aspects.

It would appear that there are two options in relation to the Popkess Affair, dependent on which side the investigator comes down on, or perhaps their political persuasion.

On the one hand, Owen and Wigman cite the rather serendipitous timing of numerous separate investigations into the Council all within a short space of time; that time being immediately prior to local elections where the publication of the allegations would do the most harm. These investigations were also conducted in the period immediately after the Council had refused Popkess money to incept his much-vaunted Traffic Wardens initiative, as well as their stalwart refusal to provide any further police housing. It is easy to see how this set of circumstances led them to conclude that Popkess, approaching retirement and with comparatively little to lose, had set about on a crusade to discredit certain persons in the Council who had wronged him in some way.

The opposing view which the Council ultimately seemed to accept in the light of the subsequent investigation and DPP conclusions is that actually Alderman Wigman was sailing close to the wind of legitimacy. His dictatorial style of leadership, backed up by a close circle of loyal subordinates, enabled him to undertake nefarious activities that he believed he could get away with because no-one would either report them or investigate them. He was then aided and sheltered, either intentionally or accidentally, by Owen, who had a strong personality and stubborn opinions over his role and that of the police. Certainly, all the issues that brought about Popkess' suspension boil down to the investigation into the activities of Wigman, who himself initiated the suspension of the Chief Constable after removing the key person who opposed it and could have blocked it, in Alderman Coffey.

The ultimate conclusion of the Popkess Affair, in conjunction with several other slightly less high-profile national policing

146

scandals, was the inception of a Royal Commission into Policing. The Royal Commission was issued with four terms of reference for its purview, the first two of which almost certainly stemmed primarily from The Popkess Affair, those being:

1) The constitution and functions of local police authorities

2) The status and accountability of members of police forces, including the Chief Officers of Police.

Popkess provided a submission to the Committee, and many of the documents relating to the Popkess Affair formed part of the evidence they heard, including the letter from Popkess to the DPP outlining the case against Wigman and the DPP's response. One outcome of the Royal Commission was clearly a direct result of the Affair, with Recommendation 15 proposing that Watch Committees be empowered to request reports from their Chief Constable, but that those Chiefs, with agreement from the Home Office, could refuse to provide them. Another recommendation also changed the structure of Watch Committees, transforming them into Police Authorities and ensuring that they comprised at least a third of Justices of the Peace (Magistrates) free from political allegiance.

A sad aside in relation to the Royal Commission was that as he was gathering his evidence, The Captain wrote to his replacement in the Nottingham City Police, Thomas Moore, asking for documents relating to the Affair. On 17th March 1961 Moore wrote back to Popkess explaining that he "cannot possibly accede to your request" as he felt "it would be a most improper thing for me to do and would place me in a most embarrassing position". Moore cited the goodwill and renewed relationship that the force had built with the Council in the intervening year as the reason for this. His letter is clearly tinged with sadness, with

Moore addressing his former mentor and boss with "Dear Pop", clearly showing the very close relationship the two men had. It does demonstrate that the force and the Council had moved on and put the matter behind them, leaving only the embattled and scapegoated former mighty Chief Constable still trying to make his case.[91]

Such renewed relationships weren't felt by everyone, however, with the rank-and-file officers clearly incensed at the actions of the Council. Bob Rosamund recalls that there was "fury" over the Popkess Affair. He explains that "Everyone knew the Council were fiddling. Trouble is, Popkess told them so." Rosamund is in no doubt that the matter broke Popkess' heart, to be treated in the way he was after all he'd done for the city, and that it put a stain over the end of The Captain's great career. As a result, he says, officers looked to "do the Council for any offences" such as Road Traffic matters or anything else.

Popkess himself was not one for forgiveness and moving on either. After his exoneration, reinstatement and subsequent retirement, he was firmly resolved to sue the Nottingham City Council and to "have his day in court". It was only the intervention of a character almost the antithesis of Popkess that managed to dissuade Popkess from following that route.

The secretary of the Association of Chief Police Officers, Chief Constable of Hertfordshire Albert 'Michael' Wilcox, was an academic, gentleman and veteran of the very first cohort of 'high potential training' at Hendon. He was also fortuitously someone who was adamantly opposed to the interference of politics in policing. He noted in his unpublished memoirs that "in my mind

91 National Archives 272/83 Letter from Thomas Moore to Captain A Popkess 17th March 1961. And Bowley "The Popkess Affair" p.184

Popkess was undoubtedly right [in his refusal to comply with the Watch Committee]".

Wilcox also wrote that Popkess was a "rather headstrong character" who wasn't going to simply sit back and wait for the Home Office to intervene over his suspension. Wilcox presumably did not know about Popkess' previous successes with such direct action, but being of more a cautious nature he was not so sure about such an approach himself. This was also a very public incident, making national news. He therefore instructed a solicitor to review the case on behalf of ACPO, who were fully prepared to back Popkess' standpoint.

The ACPO solicitor was confident that Popkess would win in any litigation, but Wilcox and his fellow Chief Constable John Peel of Essex, the ACPO chairperson, were still fearful that "much dirty laundry would be washed in public". There would also likely be severe reputational damage to Popkess and the Police Service (and to a lesser degree from their perspective Nottingham City Council) from any additional information that came out in court, as well as a resuming of the previous public slanging match.

In order to dissuade Popkess from this course of action, Wilcox invited him to stay with him at his home in Hertfordshire. There Popkess regaled Wilcox's son with tales from his childhood in South Africa, which understandably thrilled the young man. During this sojourn, Wilcox managed to persuade Popkess not to embark on his desired course of action, and instead to let the matter rest. He wrote of the incident that the £275 fee paid to the solicitor out of ACPO funds was "money well spent".[92] This was

92 Emsley, Clive: *A Police Officer and a Gentleman: A. F 'Michael' Wilcox* London: Blue Lamp Books (2018) p. 171 and unpublished notes by Wilcox, Michael pp. 2 – 5 courtesy of private correspondence with Clive Emsley.

in spite of the Association barely having the funds at that time to cover this expense, and having to consider taking out an overdraft to cover it. The views of the entire organisation, however, were unanimously in support of Popkess and the use of its funds in this way to answer the key constitutional question regarding the position of Constables (and most importantly Chief Constables) with regards to local Corporations.[93]

Bob Rosamund is certainly correct that the Affair put a significant dampener on Popkess' retirement. It could be argued, however, that it in fact ensured a small spotlight remained on this great man, giving his name to a small but significant part of policing history.

It is a tragedy that his name is associated with this negative incident, when it should be linked to any one of his myriad innovations.

93 Hull History Centre ACPO archive UDPO/10/756b Letter from Cyril Carter to N.W Goodchild 5th October 1959 and Extract from the Minutes of a meeting of the ACPO Executive Committee held on 21st January 1960.

10.

FINAL THOUGHTS

It is quite staggering that an individual who pioneered so many changes in the police service through his innovations is almost unknown apart from the eponymous incident that gained him notoriety. Even that small fame is largely confined to a small number of police history books. Hopefully, the evidence in this book should be obvious in support of just how important and influential a figure Captain Athelstan Popkess was to policing in the Twentieth and Twenty-First Centuries.

Indeed, there is a strong case to be made that no one other person has made more of a contribution to British policing since the founding triumvirate of Sir Robert Peel, Charles Rowan and Richard Mayne. Certainly, no single person did more to advance the technology in policing and, as was argued in the chapter The Mechanized Division, Popkess' introduction of that department more than anything else marks the watershed moment between Victorian-era 'beat' policing and modern 'mobile' or 'response' policing.

Why then is he not better known?

Had Popkess been in the Metropolitan Police his achievements would have likely been lauded by Parliament and replicated nationally. The history of policing in Britain, as with many other facets of society, is heavily London-centric. With the Metropolitan Police having an officer number equivalent to most of the 'rural' forces combined, it is not necessarily surprising. The seat of the British Government is in London, and as such the Metropolitan Police act as exemplars of UK policing in the eyes of those in power.

The recent example of Operation Yewtree and its derivatives demonstrated that when the Metropolitan Police kept high profile personages on bail for lengthy periods the Government changed the law to protect their own. It wasn't that people hadn't been kept on bail for long periods before, it was simply that it was now happening to 'the man', and as such the law was changed. Consider this analogy extended say to Traffic Wardens. Had Popkess introduced Traffic Wardens patrolling the streets of London ensuring less congestion around the Palace of Westminster and its environs, how quickly would this idea have been mandated across the country?[94] This is just the example of Traffic Wardens. How much more advanced would the national police service be now if this had been the case for all Popkess' innovations, rather than other forces only becoming aware through his writings and adopting them in a haphazard way? How much further along would the Metropolitan Police be if Popkess had introduced the Mechanized Division there rather than Nottingham, some decade or so before they reached the same level of ability with two-way radio transmissions and fast response? Instead, he was the head of a relatively small provincial borough police force, so his tenure passed by almost unnoticed.

Perhaps it is the nature of the Public Sector that 'best practice' initiatives are simply adopted by other Public Sector bodies

92 Albeit, what might be the alternate consequences if MPs regularly received tickets...

(other police forces) and no credit is given. In private industry, Popkess would likely have been a figure very similar to Apple's Steve Jobs: aloof and introverted to a large degree, locking himself away to develop his ideas, being socially awkward and holding hundreds of patents for his initiatives – and therefore receiving credit along the lines of other significant innovators.

There is also a case to be made that Popkess was somewhat of a Nikola Tesla figure, with ideas almost too advanced for his time, resulting in him being seen as some kind of quack or eccentric, but who now, decades later, has had his work vindicated through technological and social progress. Certainly, this is the case for The Captain's work on drink driving and speed cameras, and to a lesser extent driver behaviour as a whole. Popkess' 'vilification' is not to the same degree as Tesla's (who died destitute and hounded out by his peers), because many of his ideas did gain universal favour and became adopted quickly on a national scale.

He did, however, retire very soon after his 'discrediting' and almost immediately left Nottingham, relocating to Torquay, Devon, with the intention of writing his children's books, and perhaps returning to South Africa. The only thing from Nottingham that he took, according to his former staff officer Dennis Silverwood, was his manservant.

After suffering terribly from lumbago which could render him almost paralysed for days, Popkess died there only eight years later on 1st May 1967; luckily for him, a year before his pride and joy – Nottingham City Police – was merged with its County neighbour to form Nottinghamshire Combined Constabulary.

Perhaps, as is inevitable with all such characters who believe so passionately in what they are doing, they will always be ultimately 'hounded out' by those with grudges or differences of opinion and a modicum of power enabling them to do so. Steve Jobs was fired from his own company by the board who couldn't tolerate his 'driven' attitude, focussing on what he believed was the right course of action. Similarly, Popkess was ousted by the City Council when he was acting in his capacity as a police officer to investigate an allegation into them, when he refused to kowtow to their demands. Ultimately, both men returned to their positions, but due to Popkess' advanced age by that time, coupled with his depression, he lacked the strength and will to continue. Instead, he chose to retire and leave on his terms.

It is incredibly sad that such an earth-moving individual was all-but forced out by a relatively minor bureaucrat, who felt that he was more important than he actually was. For his life's work and considerable achievements to be undermined in such a manner, and having to suffer the ignominy of being suspended most likely brought about his premature death. This is exacerbated by the fact that Capt Popkess was demonstrably a prideful man, as can be evidenced repeatedly by his recruitment criteria, dress and behaviour standards, and his desire to always publish his excellent work to highlight it to the wider policing community.

As a somewhat alternative viewpoint, however, upon Popkess' retirement both the President and Honorary Secretary of the Association of Chief Police Officers felt that the last year of Popkess' career was his most defining time. The Honorary Secretary, Chief Constable Norman Goodchild, described how Popkess "performed your greatest service of all to the Police Force in the stand you took and the splendid dignity with which you carried yourself from beginning to end." Chief Constable John Peel, the President of the Association, agreed, writing that "nothing of all you achieved became you better that your fine example in the troubles and difficulties which attended your retirement. It will long stand as an inspiration to policemen – especially to those on whom rests the responsibility of command".[95]

History, however, largely overlooks a person's bearing and behaviours, and has a tendency to examine the cold, hard facts of incidents, which on the surface at least left Popkess open to a suggestion of criticism over the Affair.

***

It is a commonly known fact within their occupation that police officers have the shortest life expectancy after retirement. This is put down to their working lives being so constantly intense only to then suddenly stop completely in retirement. This was probably even truer for Popkess than most others, as demonstrated by the en-suite bedroom next to his office which meant he didn't even have to go home. Going from being almost a hero to his peers, his subordinates and the people of the City who turned out in their thousands to demand his reinstatement to something of a 'zero', suffering the ignominy of being suspended followed by retirement and having nothing to focus his active mind on most likely contributed significantly to his early death. It is almost inconceivable now for there to be a large-scale public protest in support of a senior police officer, but such was the great respect that the City of Nottingham held Popkess in that they had turned out in their thousands to do just that.

Could he or would he have gone on for another few years had the Popkess Affair not occurred? It is impossible to say either

95 Hull History Centre ACPO Archives UDPO/10/775c Letter from John Peel to Athelstan Popkess 7th December 1959 and Hull History Centre ACPO Archives UPDO/10/775c Letter from Norman Goodchild to Athelstan Popkess 5th December 1959

way, as he was approaching retirement age regardless and had already indicated his desire to retire. He perhaps would have stayed in post long enough to oversee the introduction of the Traffic Wardens, who ultimately started work on 20th January 1964, but this may have been a lot sooner without the distractions of the Popkess Affair and then his retirement.

It is highly probable, however, that he would not have wanted to remain in post as soon as discussions around a merger with the County force began being mooted. It must also be remembered that he was evidently suffering from depression, and this would have also weighed heavily on his decision on how long to remain in post. His choice to leave Nottingham completely on retirement and move to Torquay – a town which now brands itself as the 'English Riviera' due to having the most days of sunshine per year on average, but to which he had no connection previously – would appear to support this assertion that his depression weighed heavily on him.

It seems most likely that, given a free choice and lacking the year-long distraction with the Council, he may have remained until the early 1960s to see in his new Traffic Wardens, to retire soon after on the subsequent success 'high'.

As it was, Popkess was all but forced into retirement. He didn't even get to leave on any form of high or to any celebration in recognition of his service and achievements. According to former PC Bob Rosamund, "he left without any fanfare. He just disappeared one day." He was succeeded by his Deputy Chief Constable Thomas Moore, who carried on in much the same vein, seeing through Popkess' work for eight-and-a-half years until stepping down upon amalgamation with the County force.

The case has been strongly made to honour Captain Athelstan

Popkess with the credit of being the most influential figure in British Policing since the Peel-Rowan-Mayne triumvirate, perhaps single-handedly transforming it from the Victorian beat system to the modern responsive, mobile model. Of course, as with all forms of evolution, several of Popkess' undertakings developed in parallel across other forces or pre-date his development of them. But where the credit is being given to him, it is because he had the wherewithal to adopt, adapt and develop other people's ideas from around the world, pairing them with his own initiatives, to wholly transform the Nottingham City force and British Policing as a whole.

It is also entirely probable that no one single person could hope to make such an impact on policing again. The structures, responsibilities and laws in existence now simply don't allow Chief Constables to be so removed from the running of their forces as Popkess was, thereby not allowing them time to conceive and develop ideas in the way he did. Similarly, technology today is sufficiently more advanced that a force would find it almost impossible to develop such a leap forward 'in house' as Popkess did with wireless radios and forensics. It may therefore be that no one single person, certainly in the position of a non-Metropolitan force Chief Constable, may have chance to have such a seismic impact on policing as Popkess did.

It is similarly hard to envisage a Chief Constable of the future being as impactive as was he for a variety of other reasons, not least being that the average tenure for Chiefs is now around five years or less, compared to Popkess' near 30. Current Chiefs, by law, are also required to have completed service at every rank below Chief Officer level and are therefore significantly indoctrinated in current laws, policies and procedures. Popkess came from outside policing, straight into a position where he could implement and effect change and impose his own ideas on his own force, and then encourage that change nationwide through his publications. Fortunately for Nottingham City Police, and the British Police Service as a whole, Popkess' ideas proved to be unequivocal successes; the majority, if not totality of which, are still in common usage today, 60 years after his retirement.

This impact has been forgotten over time, but certainly appears to have been understood at the time of his service by Popkess' immediate peer group of Chief Constables. On 7th December 1959 the President of the Association of Chief Police Officers wrote to Popkess to wish him well in his retirement. Such letters appeared to be customary from the ACPO president to outgoing chief officers but, tellingly, all other examples from the time appear to be pro-forma letters with the same text. Popkess received a personal letter from Chief Constable John Peel in which he praised Popkess for the "magnificent contributions you have made to the Service in general", and described how Popkess' had been "an outstanding career" in which he "made an enormous contribution to the advancement of policemanship." He relates how there were a handful of Chief Constables who "remember your earlier pioneering days and how far ahead of the times you were in your conception of modern police work."[96]

Such glowing recognition and praise from one's own peer group, and especially a peer group of experts at the top of their profession, even if taken in isolation, must mark Popkess out as being something special. Couple this with everything else discussed herein, and it is therefore the almost inevitable conclusion that Capt Athelstan Popkess CBE, OStJ, KPM was the

96 Hull History Centre ACPO Archives UDPO/10/775c Letter from John Peel to Athelstan Popkess 7th December 1959

greatest Chief Constable of the Twentieth Century, and perhaps the greatest Chief Constable since the Metropolitan Police's founding pairing of Rowan and Mayne.

The eminent police historian Richard Cowley, in his last article for the *Journal of the Police History Society*, writing about the first ever appointed Her Majesty's Inspector of Constabulary, William Cartwright, concludes with the following:

> "These benefits [of his initiatives], because they are commonplace in today's police service, are taken so much for granted that they seem scarcely worthy of interest. But when Cartwright had felt the need to propose them ... they were radical ideas, previously unvoiced.
>
> Proper perceptions such as those were essential for the proper development of the ... police service. And with his energy, astute observations, knowledge and above all, interest [he] was as much a pioneer of today's ... police service as the likes of Peel, Rowan, [and] Mayne."[97]

Whilst Cowley was writing about Cartwright, the words are just as equally true of Popkess and his innovations, some hundred years later; his innovations being so revolutionary at the time but, as highlighted, commonplace today. Surely, if there is a standard by which individual greatness is judged, it must be this contemporary innovation which becomes the standard still used decades later.

---

97 Cowley, Richard 'The First HMI: The Life and Times of William Cartwright: HM Inspector of Constabulary 1856-1869' in *Journal of the Police History Society* No. 31 (2017) p. 5

APPENDICES

COPIES OF ALL NEWSPAPER REPORTS PERTAINING TO THE TRAFFIC MANAGEMENT AROUND THE ALDERSHOT TATTOO 1929

The London *Times*, 24th June 1929

"The queen, with Prince George, and Princess Mary occupied the Royal Box. It would not be an over estimate to place the total company present at 90,000. Nearly 10,000 Motor Vehicles were parked yet the Parking places were cleared of all but picknickers within an hour and a half of the conclusion of the Tattoo"

The London *Daily Mirror*, 20th June 1929

'Traffic Marvels of the Great Tattoo'

"To me the feature of the great Searchlight Tattoo at Aldershot is the amazingly efficient organisation which extends for miles around the actual display. The huge Car Parks and the footways to the arena, cover an enormous space and are controlled by the co-operation of Police Civil and Military with a skill that creates simple order where there would otherwise be chaos. On the Way to London the traffic is controlled as far out as Sunningdale."

The London *Daily News*, 24th June 1929

'Tattoo Record'

"Just as this greatest of all Aldershot Tattoos was a triumph of showmanship, so was the dispatch of assemblies which, all told, totalled 307,400 people, a triumph of organisation, for the carrying out of which the credit may be allotted to Captain A. Popkess (Chief of Aldershot's Military Police), Superintendent W.F Jacobs (Chief of the Civil Police). Mr W. Fitt (R.A.C) and their subordinates. The Metropolitan Area itself could not find a better detachment of traffic controllers. There were 9,000 more motor vehicles and 70,000 more visitors that at last year's Tattoo, but car parks were evacuated and enclosures cleared each night, pn the average in 40% less time."

The London *Daily Mail*, 21st June 1929

'Tattoo Crowds; Impressive system of
Marshalling; Traffic without a block'

"A detached observer at the scene of the Tattoo, must have marvelled as much at the spectacle provided by the assembling; as of the show itself. Both are magnificently impressive; both are wonders of organisation. Military Police at a hundred points direct the traffic, no blocks occur nor are the pedestrians permitted to wander from the carefully mapped out routes. There is no confusion; the mighty throngs fit into their positions with the ease of an ordinary audience filling a Theatre. Afterwards the spectators disperse with the wonderful orderliness which characterises their gathering. The routes are again filled with marching hosts and thousands of motors glide away in all directions, as easily as they arrive."

The London *Daily Telegraph*, 20th June 1929

"Not the least remarkable of the many wonders connected with the Aldershot Searchlight Tattoo, are the further perfected arrangements which have been made this year for the handling of the road traffic.

The authorities are to be warmly congratulated on the scheme which they have evolved for the accommodating some 15,000 motors, and for the efficiency with which Civil and Military Police on the roads direct the incoming streams. The public are only required to affix the appropriate card to their Cars, and the Police do the rest. On the return journey the Cars were diverted with remarkable efficiency on to the various main roads, by which it was possible to make the return journey to London with equal rapidity."

The London *Daily Express*, 24th June 1929

'Triumph of Organisation; Call for superlatives'

"Until Saturday night I was convinced that the greatest organiser of out-door crowds was the late Tex Rickard, and I thought that a mark had been set at Philadelphia and Chicago that would never perhaps be approached again. I went to the Aldershot Tattoo and I now want it put on record as the maker of the statement that the man responsible for arrangements there, pushed Rickard out of sight. The Show was over at 12. How the thousands of parked Cars were sorted out and put on the road is more than I can explain, but I do know that I was back in London before 2 o'clock in the morning."

COPIES OF ALL RADIO MESSAGE EXAMPLES IN 'NOTTINGHAM CITY POLICE WIRELESS'

Date and time	
14.7.33	From H.Qs. to No.6 Patrol
14.33	2 men Harrington Drive offering to buy sovereigns for 32/6 each.
14.55	From No. 6 Patrol to H.Qs
	Have interviewed 2 men and am satisfied with their explanation.
17.7.33	From H.Qs to No.4 Patrol
21.27	Go 17 Mapperley Hall Drive break-in
21.37	From No. 4 Patrol to H.Qs
	No particulars for circulation waiting for C.I.D
2.8.33	From H.Qs to Patrols Nos. 1, 2, 3, 4, 5, 6 & 7
17.15	166 Aker Street. Man seen going over wall. Surround premises.
17.30	From No. 2 Patrol to H.Qs
	Premises searched no trace of man. Resuming patrols.
3.8.33	From H.Qs to Patrols Nos. 1, 2, 3, 4, 5 & 6
21.54	Stolen from Mansfield between 21.15 and 21.20 today Wolseley Hornet R.B.7365. Action 5.B

23.18	From No. 3 Patrol to H.Qs
	Car recovered Canning Circus thieves arrested
26.8.33	From No. 2 Patrol to H.Qs
14.54	Sid Swan, 6 Watcombe Circus reports man in brown suit and cap sallow complexion acting in suspicious manner outside house. Have searched vicinity no trace. House unoccupied request attention.
16.07	From H.Qs. to No.2 Patrol
	Man seen outside 6 Watcombe Circus has been interviewed. All correct.
26.8.33	From No. 2 Patrol to H.Qs
22.38	Has been accident at Moor Bridge. Injured man being conveyed to General Hospital in Unity Bus. Am going to Hospital to inquire.
23.20	From No. 2 Patrol to H.Qs
	Made inquiries. No useful information from injured man. Resuming patrol.
31.8.33	From H.Qs. to No.1 Patrol
20.44	Proceed 33 S--- Road, and warn husband of woman who lost 2/6d that he must not threaten man once suspected of stealing it.
21.30	From No. 1 Patrol to H.Qs
	Been to disturbance. No case for police action.
31.8.33	From No. 5 Patrol to H.Qs
21.55	Re larceny of lamp. Made arrest and taken to Leenside. Making further inquiries.
6.9.33	From No. 4 Patrol to H.Qs
12.47	Am watching man in Arlington Drive will call you when I have interviewed him.
13.03	From No. 4 Patrol to H.Qs
	Have interviewed man satisfied all O.K
9.9.33	From No. 8 Patrol to H.Qs
20.52	Watching car at Greyhound Track. Further information later.

Appendix 2

21.29	From No. 8 Patrol to H.Qs
	Motor car at Greyhound Track O.K
30.9.33	From No. 1 Patrol to H.Qs
14.39	Have found child reported missing what shall I do with it?
14.41	From H.Qs. to No.1 Patrol
	Take to Hyson Green
4.10.33	From H.Qs. to Nos. 4 & 5 Patrols
22.08	Go to Samuels, Long Row, alarm bell ringing
22.19	From No. 4 Patrol to H.Qs
	O.K Samuels alarm bell short-circuiting
10.10.33	From H.Qs. to No.4 Patrol
20.09	9 Carisbrook Drive. Suspicious noises
20.19	From No. 4 Patrol to H.Qs
	Searched grounds no trace. Resuming patrol.
10.10.33	From No. 7 Patrol to H.Qs
22.38	Send ambulance to Hucknall Lane boundary serious accident
22.50	Ring County Police Hucknall to send tape measure
11.10.33	From No. 6 Patrol to H.Qs
22.19	Inform Lighting Dept. overhead lights in Wheeler Gate are out.
12.10.33	From No. 4 Patrol to H.Qs
09.41	Contact with suspected vehicle G.Y.9166 Kirkewhite Street at 09.40
09.48	Suspected vehicle now delivering Skinner and Rook Clumber Street
10.02	Suspects delivering Pullman's Parliament Street
10.18	Suspects delivering Black's Factory Sherwood Street
10.33	Suspects delivering Boulevard Works, Radford Boulevard
10.38	Suspect & receiver arrested shop Ilkeston Road. C.I.D bringing in prisoners

169

10.45	From H.Qs. to No.4 Patrol
	Resume Patrol
12.10.33	From No. 5 Patrol to H.Qs
	Traffic signal lights King Edward Street out of order
13.10.33	From H.Qs. to No.4 Patrol
	Indecent exposure outside school Woodborough Road. Get in touch with area man and work in conjunction with him.
13.10.33	From H.Qs. to Patrols Nos. 1, 2 & 4
13.15	Walk-in Woodborough Rd. Man described age 35 5'6" slim build, C.S long thin face. Mouth sunk. Grey suit & cap. Patrol vicinity.
14.17	From No. 4 Patrol to H.Qs
	No trace walk-in
14.19	From H.Qs. to Nos. 1, 2 & 4 Patrols
	Return patrol areas
14.10.33	From H.Qs. to No.4 Patrol
23.29	Man loitering Chestnut Grove
23.49	From No. 4 Patrol to H.Qs
	Taking man loitering into C.I.D for interrogation
15.10.33	From No. 3 Patrol to H.Qs
23.33	Am standing by for communication purposes at big fire Basford

ABOUT THE AUTHOR

My personal interest in Capt Popkess was first piqued when I was given a copy of *Nottingham City Police: A Pictorial History 1930–1960* by PC David (Dan) Hyndman as a gift. Given the book's timespan (concurrent to the stewardship of Capt Popkess), the book is in part hagiographical towards him, and he features heavily in the images within. I was intrigued. The pictures in the book, although from only 50 years ago, showed a force of Police Officers who were at a pinnacle of national and international sporting achievement. Officers who wore their uniforms with pride and earned respect from colleagues and public alike. This in my mind stood in stark contrast to the Police Force of today, where officers are largely forbidden from undertaking anything but police work during their duties; who distance themselves from the profession during their everyday lives and to whom occasionally uniform standards appear all but uniform or standard. PC Hyndman's book therefore ignited a spark of interest in me to know more about why and how a British Police Force became renowned internationally for sporting achievements, and how some of its officers became local household names.

With a degree in History behind me, and an ongoing active interest in both current and historical policing, I undertook some more research, reading and discussion with like-minded colleagues into Capt Popkess. The more I read, the more fascinated I was by this man's achievements and initiatives, and the more I wanted to know.

I was then encouraged to further research Capt Popkess as a result of a meeting with the then Editor of the *Journal* of the Police History Society – an organisation of which I had only been a member for a few years. I had previously submitted an article to the *Journal* that was largely based around some University work I had undertaken, then polished and updated during a period of illness from work. Richard Cowley had just taken over the Editor's position that year, and remembered reading my article the previous year, telling me that he had enjoyed it (largely because in it I had agreed with his interpretation of events in his book *A History of the British Police* over another historian's!). He asked me if I had any plans to write another, or was conducting any other research currently. Other than my passing interest into Capt Popkess, I wasn't – work and life can get in the way of things like that when you're not a full-time academic or retired – but I mentioned that I was looking into Capt Popkess and was intrigued by this enigmatic Chief of Nottingham City Police from 50 years ago. Richard was very kind and said that he'd be delighted if I wanted to write another article and submit it to him – to help ensure that he had sufficient material to publish for his first editorial effort. Over the next few months, I bought a few books, took a few trips to the library, trawled the internet, and pieced together a short-ish study into Capt Popkess, which was published in the 2016 *Journal*. Even at 3,500 words, I found that I was condensing things to a point that I was almost unhappy with in my efforts to convey the seismic impact that Capt Popkess had on British policing, and almost doing a man I had come to respect and admire, an injustice.

I did have a slight dig at PC Hyndman above, accusing him

of hagiography over his slight reverential style towards Capt Popkess, which I fully accept will be a key criticism of this book too. Perhaps though that is a necessity when writing an autobiography, as it would be a somewhat bizarre exercise and highly unusual to dedicate time and effort into producing a work about a person whom you dislike; barring perhaps particularly key controversial historical figures. I offer no apologies for this fact, however, firmly believing that Capt Popkess is deserving of significantly more recognition than he is the current recipient of; having so fundamentally changed the dynamics and structure of modern policing.

As part of my research I had the pleasure of meeting several characters who had served under Popkess and who were willing to give me their time to regale me with their anecdotes. Sadly, a few months after I interviewed him, Dennis Silverwood passed away, never having the opportunity to read this work that he contributed so significantly to. I was honoured to have provided a guard of honour at his funeral, and am delighted that a small part of his memories are recorded in these pages. Bob Rosamund too was of great help to me, providing me with pictures and ongoing support throughout my time writing.

Finally, I am aware of the possible existence of a draft manuscript written by Capt Popkess entitled 'Chapter's End' that he had intended to be a follow-up to *Guns in the Sun* detailing his time serving in Ireland. This was previously in the archive at the Open University, but this collection was disbanded shortly before I started writing this work. Try as I might I have been unable to locate it for this work. Should anyone come across it at a future date, I would be delighted to know its whereabouts, allowing me to do a potentially produce a second edition to this work incorporating that new information.

BIBLIOGRAPHY

Andrews, Tom "Athelstan Popkess CBE, OStJ, KPM: The Twentieth Century's Greatest Chief Constable?" in *The Journal of the Police History Society* Vol. 30 (2016)

Bowley, Alfred S "Politicians and the Police in Nottingham: The Popkess Affair, 1959" in *Transactions of the Thoroton Society of Nottinghamshire* Vol. 108 (2004) pp 173 – 186

Bunker, John *From Rattle to Radio* Brewin Books: Surrey (1988)

Cowley, Richard *A History of the British Police: From its Earliest Beginnings to the Present Day* Gloucestershire: The History Press (2011)

Emsley, Clive *A Police Officer and a Gentleman: A. F "Michael" Wilcox* London: Blue Lamp Books (2018)

Hayes, Nick *Consensus and Controversy: City Politics in Nottingham 1945-1966* Liverpool: Liverpool University Press (1996)

Hyndman, David *Nottingham City Police: A Pictorial History 1930 – 1960* Newark: Davage Printing Ltd

Hyndman, David *Nottingham City Police: A Pictorial History 1960 – 1968* Newark: Davage Printing Ltd

Needham, David *Battle of the Flames: Nottinghamshire's fight for survival in WW II* Ashbourne, Derbyshire: The Horizon Press (2009)

Phillips, Robert & Andrews, Tom *100 Years of Women in Policing* Nottingham: Nottinghamshire Police (2015)

Popkess, Capt. Athelstan *Nottingham City Police: Centenary 1935* Nottingham: Nottingham City Police Press (1945)

Popkess, Athelstan *Traffic Control and Road Accident Prevention* Chapman & Hall (1951)

Popkess, Capt Athelstan *Sweat in My Eyes* Leicester: Edgar Backus (1952)

Popkess, Athelstan as Kidogo, Bardo *Guns in the Sun* London: Arthur H Stockwell

Popkess, Athelstan *Mechanised Police Patrol* Barnicotts Ltd: Somerset (1954)

Popkess, Athelstan "Pursuit by Wireless: The Value of Mobility" in *The Police Journal: Theory, Practice and Principles* Volume 6, 1 (1st January 1933)

Popkess, Athelstan "Nottingham City Police Wireless" in *The Police Journal: Theory, Practice and Principles* Volume 7, 2 (1st April 1934)

Popkess, Athelstan "Classification of Handwriting and Counterfeit Coins" in *The Police Journal: Theory, Practice and Principles* Volume 7, 3 (1st July 1934)

Popkess, Athelstan "Pursuit by Science" in *The Police Journal: Theory, Practice and Principles* Volume 8, 2 (1st April 1935)

Popkess, Athelstan "Police Co-Operation with a Burglar Alarm System" in *The Police Journal: Theory, Practice and Principles* Volume 21, 1 (1st January 1948)

Popkess, Athelstan "Judging Speed by Skid Marks" in *The Police Journal: Theory, Practice and Principles* Volume 22, 2 (1st April 1949)

Popkess, Athelstan "The Influence of Topography on Police Tactics" in *The Police Journal: Theory, Practice and Principles* Volume 23, 1 (1st January 1950)

Popkess, Athelstan "Murder as a Gamble" in *The Police Journal: Theory, Practice and Principles* Volume 25, 2 (1st April 1952)

Popkess, Athelstan "Morphia the Slayer" in *The Police Journal: Theory, Practice and Principles* Volume 25, 4 (1st October 1952)

Popkess, Athelstan "The Problem of Found and Stolen Bicycles" in *The Police Journal: Theory, Practice and Principles* Volume 28, 1 (1st January 1955)

Popkess, Athelstan "The Teleprinter and the Man on the Beat" in *The Police Journal: Theory, Practice and Principles* Volume 28, 2 (1st April 1955)

Popkess, Athelstan "The Drunken Driver" in *The Police Journal: Theory, Practice and Principles* Volume 29, 2 (1st April 1956)

Popkess, Athelstan "Assessing Police Establishments" in *The Police Journal: Theory, Practice and Principles* Volume 31, 2 (1st April 1958)

Popkess, Athelstan "Traffic Wardens: Food for Thought" in *The Police Journal: Theory, Practice and Principles* Volume 32, 2 (1st April 1959)

Stallion, Martin and Wall, David *The British Police: Forces and their Chief Officers 1829-2012* Hook, Hampshire: The Police History Society (2011)

Withers, Bill *Nottinghamshire Constabulary: 150 Years in Photographs* (Huddersfield: Quorn Publishing Ltd)

The Hull History Centre ACPO Archives UDPO/10/775 ACPO Membership etc

The Hull History Centre ACPO Archives UDPO/10/918 ACPO correspondence 1959 – 1961

The Hull History Centre ACPO Archives UDPO/10/756 Discipline Powers of the Watch Committee, Nottingham Case, Captain Aethelstan Popkess

The National Archives, HO 45/24711 (Notes on the appointment of Popkess)

The National Archives, HO 272/83 (Correspondence between Popkess and the Royal Commission on Police)

The Nottinghamshire Archives Account 6196

www.britishpathe.com/video/new-police-alarm-to-fight-theft-wave

www.macearchive.org/films/arp-practical-demonstration-nottingham-precautions

INDEX

Athelstan Popkess is abbreviated throughout to 'AP'
except at the start of his own index entry.

MORE POLICE HISTORY BOOKS FROM MANGO BOOKS:

A Girl in Blue: Memoirs of a Metropolitan Woman Police Officer 1967-73
Lois Willoughby-Easter

A Police Officer and A Gentleman: AF 'Michael' Wilcox
Clive Emsley

Jack and Old Jewry:
The City of London Policemen Who Hunted The Ripper
Amanda Harvey Purse

Never A Dull Moment: Memoirs of A Portsmouth Woman
Gladys Howard

Policing From Bow Street:
Principal Officers, Runners and the Patroles
Peter Kennison and Alan Cook

Remembering the Fallen. Volume I: Hampshire Constabulary 1914-1919
Hampshire Constabulary History Society

Sir Howard Vincent's Police Code 1889
Neil R A Bell and Adam Wood

Swanson: The Life and Times of a Victorian Detective
Adam Wood

The Annotated I Caught Crippen
Nicholas Connell

UK Police Roll of Remembrance
The Police Roll of Honour Trust

Undaunted: My Life as Policeman and Private Eye
Jim Smith

Blue Lamp Books is an imprint of
Mango Books

www.MangoBooks.co.uk